WITHDRAWN
FROM
STOCK

WILLIAM LAI

FOOTBALL
DARK ARTS

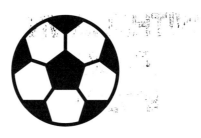

Every Crafty Trick in the Book From
Time-Wasting Tactics to Devious Deceptions

Illustrated by Jojo Chin

MEYER & MEYER SPORT

British Library Cataloguing in Publication Data
A catalogue record for this book is available from the British Library

Football Dark Arts
Maidenhead: Meyer & Meyer Sport (UK) Ltd., 2020
ISBN: 978-1-78255-201-7

© 2020 by Meyer & Meyer Sport (UK) Ltd.
Aachen, Auckland, Beirut, Cairo, Cape Town, Dubai, Hägendorf, Hong Kong, Indianapolis, Maidenhead, Manila, New Delhi, Singapore, Sydney, Tehran, Vienna

Member of the World Sport Publishers' Association (WSPA), www.w-s-p-a.org
Printed by Print Consult, GmbH, Munich, Germany

ISBN: 978-1-78255-201-7
Email: info@m-m-sports.com
www.thesportspublisher.com

CONTENTS

FOREWORD

I was asked to write a foreword to this book because I am known to be opinionated on the subject of ethics in sport, and football in particular.

By way of background, I grew up in a different time and place, which of course has shaped my personal values and philosophy. As a young kid in England, my main sport was cricket, a sport that, as etymologists will know, generated the phrase, *'it's just not cricket'* to describe any behaviour or attitude that falls below the expected norms of decency. My parents instilled in me a sense that there are only two ways to do something – the right way and the wrong way.

Everything was black or white. That is why I was, and remain, disgusted by Diego Maradona's so-called *'hand of God'* (which should have been *'hand of the devil'* in my opinion). I still find it abhorrent when somebody cheats at sport under any circumstances. So that is my unambiguous starting point.

However, I recognize that my views will appear quaint, quirky, and old-fashioned to many. I also know that events and actions in football are not always black and white. Indeed many of the 'laws' are open to interpretation.

There is often a thin line separating staying within the laws (bending them) and breaking them. With so much at stake now in terms of money, jobs, reputation, and prestige, it is not surprising that people will seek any form of competitive advantage.

This book and its clever use of examples illustrate how to do this. I have to say that some examples are more legitimate than others, but whether they are technically cheating or not, the point is that they are undoubtedly part of the game. Thus, whether you are trying to implement them or stop them, it is valid to learn about them.

One of my biggest bugbears is *'time-wasting'*. It is time to unburden my soul. To my undying shame, I was once guilty of this myself when in the semi-final of the Cheshire veterans Cup, and while winning 1-0 in added time, I *'hoofed'* the ball as far as I could out of play to delay the other team taking the throw-in. We won that match and went on to win the final, and whilst to some my negative contribution was ultimately justified, I still regret it because *'it's just not cricket'*.

I hate it when a substituted player meanders off the pitch at a pace slower than a walk to wind down the clock. This and all of the other time-wasting initiatives cited in the book could be solved at a stroke by using the 'stopwatch' system. It works perfectly well in other sports such as basketball and rugby as well as in football's sister sport, futsal. I implore IFAB to introduce it.

It is salutary to learn that experiments have shown that the ball is in play only around 60 minutes during a 90-minute match. We're all being short-changed more so when the dark arts are being performed.

So whilst I can't say I agree with the dark arts of football, I agree that, like it or not, they are part of our game. In this context I refuse to call it our *'beautiful'* game, but if you are involved in football in any capacity, it is as well to know about the dark arts, to recognize them, and to understand them.

For these reasons I commend this book to you.

Mark Sutcliffe, CEO
Hong Kong Football Association

ACKNOWLEDGMENTS

I am grateful to my students, my referee friends, my academic colleagues, new and lifelong friends, and everyone involved in the game from professionals to amateurs, and at the international and domestic levels.

Finally, I am forever grateful to my family for their support, guidance, and counsel.

INTRODUCTION

Dark arts are negative actions, either physical or psychological, that intentionally disadvantage opponents.

Everyone who watches football knows that players have always been told to play in a sporting manner. *"Play hard but play fair; Be a good sport."* We are taught to respect and shake hands with our opponents.

Yet when we see teams perform the FIFA Handshake, which officially promotes peace and fair play, and then over the following 90 minutes observe the huge torrent of cunning chicanery, rascally ruses, verbal sparring, and wily one-upmanship carried out by players and coaches on their opponents and toward match officials, it makes you wonder what is really going on out there on the pitch, on the sidelines, and in the dressing rooms.

During the match, there is much disdain for opponents, including provocation, intimidation, deliberate interruption, foul language, and other unmannerly actions and behaviours that have traditionally been censored, downplayed, and swiftly dismissed by the media and authorities. For their own reasons, the mainstream stakeholders prefer to focus primarily on the positive and sporting aspects of *the Beautiful Game.*

Officially, the dark arts are not taught, and there are no books from the football authorities that discuss or raise awareness of the dark arts. In contrast, there are plenty of manuals and online videos on soccer drills and fancy skills that promote the "beauty" in *the*

Beautiful Game. And there are of course official rulebooks and regulations that tell everyone how they must play (i.e. with fairness and integrity). But in reality, players hardly ever read the rulebooks, which are revised and released annually by the International Football Association Board (IFAB).

Yet everyone knows players dive, deceive, and double-cross in their attempt to outwit the referees and circumvent the rules. How are the negative and dirty aspects of the game taught? Players must learn the dark arts somehow and from somewhere. But there are no official manuals to teach players how to con their way to winning. And no manager, coach, or football club would ever openly admit to teaching immoral actions and using the dark arts.

Players learn about football's dark arts in exactly the same way they learn about the rules of the game. Intuition. Players spend time observing (and being duped by) successful and experienced master practitioners of the dark arts, and then they imitate the experts and hone their negative skills.

This book is the first detailed collection of its kind, revealing unofficial tricks and gamesmanship that professional players have intuitively learned since they first took to the training pitch as bright-eyed, innocent, junior players.

If you want to bend the rules and gain a winning edge over your opponents, this book's comprehensive collection of dark arts will help you. Also, if you want to understand the tricks and avoid being duped, then this book will be invaluable for you and your teammates.

This book deals with two main categories of dark arts: time-wasting and deception tactics. There is a third category dealing with how to collect cautions without causing harm to opponents or obtaining self-inflicted injuries.

Time-wasting is basically the use of unsporting methods to delay or slow down the game. Its aim is to give opponents fewer opportunities to play and hence score. There are **25 top tricks** for time-wasting.

Deception tactics are unsporting actions used to scam opponents and hoodwink match officials without getting caught and penalised. This section has **30 mischievous methods** for deceiving opponents and match officials.

The third section will help players choose the best option to deliberately obtain yellow cards should they "need" to. Without any knowledge or clear instructions about how to pick up a yellow card, players can fail spectacularly. They usually end up badly hacking down an opponent—sometimes inadvertently injuring themselves in the process—and being sent off instead of getting the intended caution. This section has **25 mellow ways** to get yellow cards without requiring players to recklessly tackle an opponent.

Never before have so many dark arts in football been collected and published. Altogether there are 80 ruses here for your perusal. The dark arts can give you and your team the slightest of winning edges, which in the modern game is all that separates winners from losers.

A little note to readers in the US: The term "football" refers to the sport "Association Football", which was established and first standardized by a group of privately schooled young gentlemen in 1863 and affectionately abbreviated by their peers as "assoccer" (in the same fashion English schoolboys used "rugger" for "Rugby Football"). This is why association football eventually became known as "soccer".

THE DARK ARTS

The first unwritten rule in football that every player learns is **never ever retrieve the ball for your opponents**.

It is learned intuitively when players, as young as 7 or 8 years old, first realize they can be made a *"chump"* or *"patsy"* (i.e. taken advantage of) if they help fetch the ball for their opponent. This first unwritten rule in football opens the path to the dark side.

By not retrieving the ball for opponents, players learn that this natural delay gives them time to catch their breath and get back into position in time for the restart. When it is the opponents' responsibility to restart the game, it is not unfair to leave the ball for them to retrieve themselves.

In itself, not retrieving the ball for opponents is not a dark art. It can be considered innocuous and *"fair game"* since this passive action is a harmless gesture, which does not actively disadvantage opponents.

However, from this basic concept comes time-wasting where players who concede a restart (like a free kick, goal kick, corner kick or a throw in) will intentionally feign to retrieve or pretend to stop a moving ball for an opponent, and then at the last moment will quickly *"change their mind about helping"* (see **TW1 False Fetch**). This is the beginning of the dark arts, where there is active intent to deceive the opponent.

From time-wasting, other dirty tricks developed that deliberately exploit weaknesses or ignorance in opponents. These tricks include provoking, intimidating and gaining an unfair advantage over opponents.

To recognise the dark arts, it is necessary to observe many of these unsavoury incidents in action. Watch online video compilations by searching for *"crazy football fights"*, *"El Clasico fights, fouls, red cards"*, and *"dirty Chelsea Tottenham 2016 fights fouls"*. Such videos demonstrate the time-wasting and devious deceptions that abound in the game and are described in this book.

A Special Understanding of the Game

José Mourinho

Love him or loathe him, José Mourinho, one the most charismatic and controversial managers in football, is a master of the dark arts.

He is an example of many stakeholders in the game who possess a pragmatic and cynical approach, which encourages an understanding and the use of the dark arts. On many occasions, Mourinho has publicly lost patience with the likes of club directors, players, medical personnel, agents, and sports journalists. This is because they lack that special understanding of the game.

In Mourinho's world, this special cynical understanding cannot be taught formally or officially. This also explains why he, and other astute and demanding managers, do not always get along with decisions made by match officials and competition administrators since officials and administrators tend to go *by the book* (i.e. they follow the official Laws of the Game and competition regulations), whereas managers and players consistently attempt to bend the rules to their own advantage.

These managers much prefer observant individuals in the game who are crafty and street smart, know how others get away with bending the rules, and who do not boast about and show off using the darks arts themselves. So when people around Mourinho *"don't get it"*, he gets mad and will not waste any more time with them.

The following three cases—toward a player, a reporter, and a medical doctor—clearly illustrate Mourinho's special understanding of the game, which he expects others around him to also possess.

First, during the 2016-2017 season when Mourinho became manager of Manchester United, he was publicly critical of promising left-back Luke Shaw. From day one, it appeared Mourinho believed Shaw did not have the right mentality and understanding of the game.

Here are Mourinho's post-match comments about Shaw:[1]

"He must understand the game; he must think, and he must accelerate the process because 21-years-old is old enough to have a better understanding of the game. I was making every decision for him. At this level we need the fantastic body he has to play football, the fantastic physical qualities he has, the very good technical ability he has, but he cannot play with my understanding of the game".

One season later, Mourinho remained frustrated with Shaw:[2]

"Luke in the first half every time they come in his corridor, the cross was coming and a dangerous situation was coming, so I was not happy with his performance".

At the start of the 2019-2020 season Mourinho, who was sacked by Manchester United midway during the previous season, continued his criticism of Shaw's lack of game intelligence.[3]

Second, even non-players working in the game *"must know football"*, otherwise they are not worthy to be in the presence of Mourinho. He infamously stormed off from a post-match interview with a BBC journalist.

The journalist was asking Mourinho to be specific about his complaints against the referee Mike Jones over Hull City's time-wasting tactics against Manchester United. Mourinho was frustrated because his team were held to a goalless draw by Hull's dark arts.

Clearly exasperated and impatient to explain his understanding of the game to a football reporter, Mourinho said:[4]

"Well if you don't know football, you shouldn't be with a microphone in your hand".

Third, the unpleasant saga with Mourinho's medical personnel, Dr Eva Carneiro and physiotherapist Jon Fearn, at Chelsea in August 2015, demonstrates how important it is for anyone around Mourinho to have his understanding of the game.

For not possessing this same understanding, the good doctor was discharged from her pitchside duties, and, in turn, she instigated unfair dismissal charges against Mourinho and her employer Chelsea. Fearn took his punishment quietly and, after a while, regained his place on the Chelsea bench.

Officially FIFA, through its medical committee, resolutely backed Carneiro's pitchside actions, which are in accordance with the Laws of the Game (i.e. *by the book*).

Furthermore the Football Medical Association, a UK group representing the interests of health professionals involved in professional football, clarified for the record that when a player is injured it is the duty of the referee to permit medical assessment and evaluation.

> *"At that moment the player becomes a patient of the medical team, and it is the duty and obligation of club medical staff to attend to that patient accordingly and without prejudice to the interests of anyone else, including the club employing them."*

Dr Eva Carneiro

Nevertheless, despite this clear stance on the rules for medical treatment on the pitch, Mourinho does not care. To him, rules are meant to be bendable and breakable.

Here's how Mourinho explained his way of thinking:[5]

"I wasn't happy with my medical staff because even if you are a medical doctor or secretary on the bench, you have to understand the game. If you go to the pitch to assist a player, then you must be sure that a player has a serious problem. I was sure that Eden didn't have a serious problem. He had a knock and was very tired. My medical department left me with eight fit outfield players in a counterattack after a set piece, and we were worried we didn't have enough players left."

To Mourinho, his medical crew were naive because they put the whole team in jeopardy during the closing stages of the match. By entering the pitch and thereby having to take Hazard off the pitch, they had stupidly given a significant numerical advantage of nine versus eleven players to their opponents.

Mourinho knew his player was wasting time and refuses to accept that his medical team did not know.

It does not matter that according to the laws and regulations Carnerio was correct in following her duties and that Mourinho was wrong. It does not matter that Carneiro was genuinely concerned about the welfare of her club's player Eden Hazard and not the score. It does not matter that referee Michael Oliver signalled, not once but twice, to the Chelsea bench that medical assistance was required by their player. It does not matter that eventually Carneiro won out-of-court damages worth over £1.2 million (approximately $1.5 million).

What matters is that if you want to be in Mourinho's company, and if you want to be a winner, then you must understand the game's dark arts. Carneiro, a medical practitioner, is perhaps too nice and naïve to be considered a practitioner of the dark arts.

This book is about the dark arts and its master practitioners. Mourinho is specifically mentioned because he is effectively the *"extra player"* of his teams. His arrogance, charisma, and bold statements allow him to get inside his opponents' heads, and sometimes also the match officials' heads. Mourinho cleverly uses the dark arts to motivate his own team, while simultaneously undermining his opponents through psychological and, on occasion, physical means.

Managers like Mourinho prefer smart players who can instinctively learn things quickly. They follow instructions, do what is asked of them, maintain fitness, and keep a low profile off the pitch.

In Patrick Barclay's biography of Mourinho,[6] he said the manager will easily *"cast aside those he perceives to be of faint heart or unsuitable head"*. Aside from Shaw, Anthony Martial is another example of a player who Mourinho perceived to be "mentally weak".[7]

When asked who his favourite players were during his time managing at Chelsea, Inter Milan and Real Madrid, Mourinho replied:[8]

"People like Marco Materazzi, Javier Zanetti, Frank Lampard, Didier Drogba, John Terry, Xabi Alonso, Arbeloa ... they give everything they can. Guys who were born to be at that level, born to be team

men. Not the ego. Not super-quality as a player in some cases – but team men. The manager's right arm."

There are of course other *"right arm"* players Mourinho preferred, such as Sergio Ramos, Ricardho Carvalho and Pepe, who are recognised masters of the dark arts.

And Paulo Ferreira, prised from Porto as soon as Mourinho was installed as Chelsea manager in 2004, is another *"right arm"* described as *"a player who will never be man of the match but will always score 7/10 for his individual display"*.

These then are players who follow orders, do their job well, go home, return, and repeat this over and over. Their realistic understanding of the game, consistent execution of their responsibilities, and awareness of the dark arts are what Mourinho and other similar managers require of them.

As a manager with a special understanding of the game, Mourinho makes things easier for his players. For instance, the level of detail that goes into his scouting reports of the opposition permits every player in Mourinho's squad to know exactly what they must do to give them the best chance of winning.

The revelation of the extensive notes compiled when Mourinho's Chelsea faced Barcelona in the last-16 Champions League match in 2006 demonstrate how calculated, strategic, and premeditated are Mourinho's actions.[9] Mourinho's instructions to his players in 2006 regarding an 18-year-old Lionel Messi was to *"Foul him ... outside the box and as early as possible"*. Chelsea's Asier del Horno clearly heeded his manager's instructions and was sent off after 36 minutes for a studs-up, high-footed challenge into Messi's thigh.

Ultimately, players and managers like those described here are all winners. They understand the dark arts are an important aspect of the game that—while not guaranteeing them a win every time—will always give them a competitive edge over those who ignore, or who remain ignorant of, the dark arts.

The dark arts exist, and we ignore them at our peril.

1 TIME-WASTING TACTICS

. . . .

Time-wasting is a dark art. It typically rears its ugly head towards the end of the first half, and also towards the end of the match when one team wants to maintain the status quo in their favour. This means if a team is content with the current score (i.e. they are all square or are in the lead), then they will *"run down the clock"* with the following *"unwritten rules"* described in this chapter.

The aim of **running down the clock** is to keep possession and to pause, slow down, or delay the actual playing time, so the opposition has fewer opportunities to play the ball and score.

Identifying when time-wasting occurs is simple. Just take note of how a team normally restarts play when they are playing and actually trying to get a result. There is a marked difference in the *"eagerness and willingness to play"* when a team genuinely wants to compete and when a team just wants to waste time.

During time-wasting, a bonus is to goad opponents and their supporters, so those with a short temper might react unreasonably, which can further delay proceedings.

For instance, players can react angrily by withholding the ball from opponents. This can lead to arguments, mass confrontations, and result in the referee meting out disciplinary actions. Additionally, supporters can be provoked into throwing objects like firecrackers or flares onto the pitch leading to delays or even temporary suspension in play.

Hence, the dark art of time-wasting comes in various forms.

> *"Mourinho's Chelsea used every trick in the book, from not giving the ball back to tying laces, going down injured and taking time from set pieces."*

—Martin Keown, football pundit, after Chelsea won 2-0 against Liverpool in 2014.

Martin Keown listed only four tricks,[10] which is not even close to the 80 tricks in this book! This first section lists 25 top tricks related to the dark art of time-wasting.

PLAYER TIME-WASTING

TW1 FALSE FETCH

TW1 DARK ART DESCRIPTION: The most basic action is to pretend to retrieve a ball for an opponent, and then at the last moment leave the ball untouched. Most players shape their body language to move as though they are stopping the ball, or bending down to pick up the ball, for their opponents. So when the ball approaches a player who wants to waste time, the player simply pretends to catch or stop the ball for their opponent who is also chasing and approaching the ball. However, instead of trapping the ball for his opponent, the player leaves it or allows it to roll on past.

VARIATIONS: One variation is to reach the ball first and then cheekily manoeuvre the ball away from the approaching opponent, such as back-heeling the ball away.

Another variation is to anticipate a collision with the opponent as the ball rolls past and then feign injury as in **TW2 Invisible Minor Injury** and **TW3 Crazy Crybabies**.

BENEFIT/CONSEQUENCES:
This basic dark art serves to delay restart and can provoke opponents.

TW2 INVISIBLE MINOR INJURY

TW2 DARK ART DESCRIPTION: Whenever the ball goes out, a player can delay the restart of play by faking injury and falling to the ground. Referees will not restart play until they personally go over and check on *"fallen"* players. As soon as the referee approaches

the player and asks whether he needs medical treatment (which also means the player must leave the pitch before play restarts), the *"injured"* player will say *"no"* and slowly get back up and stay on the pitch. This is all it takes to delay putting the ball back into play.

BENEFIT/CONSEQUENCES: Beware time-wasters!

Frustrated opponents have been known to carry off time-wasters by themselves. Time-wasters risk being unceremoniously dumped off the pitch, and this could lead to a mass confrontation of players, which can further delay restart!

ONLINE SEARCH: *"carries injured player off pitch"*

There are some examples where frustrated opponents have manhandled and carried off players who are wasting time.

In England, West Ham captain Mark Noble carried off Manchester United midfielder Ander Herrera.[11]

In Egypt, an opponent carries off a time-waster pretending to have suffered an injury near the touchline in the 90th minute of a match.[12]

TW3 CRAZY CRYBABIES

TW3 DARK ART DESCRIPTION: Players can pretend to be seriously injured during a fair challenge or a minor collision. This is another technique to run down the clock because the whole exaggerated *"song and dance show"* can take a while. First, a player goes down and cries for help (either during play or when the ball goes out). Next, the referee approaches and asks whether medical attention is needed. The player will delay answering as long as possible. Then the player will say he needs help. Medical staff will come on to assess him. After another short delay, the medical staff will tell the referee that a stretcher is needed. The referee will give a signal to the stretcher-bearers. As soon as the stretcher arrives, most

players will usually get up on their own two feet and slowly walk off by themselves. By slowly and gingerly walking off the pitch rather than being swiftly carried off on a stretcher, restart is further delayed.

The player knows that as soon as he is off the pitch, the referee will whistle for restart, and then the player will immediately yell and shout at the referee to allow him to enter the pitch again (with no sign of any lasting effect of the *"injury"*).

BENEFIT/CONSEQUENCES: The overacting may provoke opponents to harry the referee about getting the *"injured"* player off the pitch, so play can continue. This might further delay the proceedings because, as far as the referee is concerned, he has to check the *"injured"* player first.

ONLINE SEARCH: *"football play acting"* or *"football fake injury"* Here is an example of a player, Danko Lazovic, playacting and pretending to be seriously injured.[13]

TW4 SNAZZY SHOWBOAT

TW4 DARK ART DESCRIPTION: To keep possession of the ball, a player can *"showboat"*. The main reason why players showboat is to waste time. Flashy skills like excessive *keepy-uppies* or standing on the ball are not usually performed during regular match play because they don't advance a team's positional and attacking strength. Therefore performing them is obviously a time-wasting tactic.

BENEFIT/CONSEQUENCES: Beware time-wasters!

While fans may enjoy some flash trickery and ball juggling skills in the public arena, fellow professional players and opposition fans will feel slighted or dissed and may take matters into their own hands (or feet)! Showboaters risk being injured from aggressive tackles, but this dark art also helps their team by forcing the referee caution or dismiss an overzealous opponent and causing a dely. Plus the added time it takes to receive medical treatment!

ONLINE SEARCH: *"showboat skills"* or *"showboating football"*.

The Orlando Pirates are leading 2-0 against Kaizer Chiefs in South Africa. So during injury time, Pirates midfielder Thabo Rakhale did some showboating and managed to provoke his opponents.[14]

TW5 FAKER TAKER THROW-IN

TW5 DARK ART DESCRIPTION: At a throw-in for the team who wants to run down the clock, a player will pick up the ball and pretend he is about to take the throw-in. Holding the ball over and behind his head, he delays and stops to give the impression he has no options to throw the ball to teammates. Then finally a teammate will approach him, whereupon he will drop the ball for his teammate to take the throw-in and run back on the pitch.

BENEFIT/CONSEQUENCES: By getting opponents switched on when appearing to take a throw-in and then slowing the game down by dropping the ball and walking away, this deflates and frustrates opponents. However, referees who are alert to this time-wasting tactic during the latter stages of a match will usually caution the first player who deliberately delayed the restart.

TW6 THROW-IN NOT IN

TW6 DARK ART DESCRIPTION: A player executes a throw-in up the field along the touchline and deliberately ensures the ball does not enter or land inside the pitch. He relies on the assistant referee to raise his flag and inform the referee that the ball did not go in to play. The throw-in must therefore be taken again from the same place, since technically the ball never actually entered the field of play. Further delay can occur if the ball has to be retrieved and returned to the thrower.

BENEFIT/CONSEQUENCES: Beware of swirling winds, which could blow the ball onto the pitch, ensuring that there won't be a delay. Or the ball may enter the pitch and then be blown out of the pitch, in which case it is the opponents who take the thrown-in at the place where the ball last left the pitch.

TW7 THROW-IN FINGERPOINTER

TW7 DARK ART DESCRIPTION: A thrower retrieves the ball and bounces it several times as he walks up to the touchline, gaining several metres from where the ball originally left the pitch. He looks at the referee and points further forward up field to ask where to take the throw-in. The referee will either tell the thrower to hold his position or even move the thrower back several metres, all of which will delay restart as the thrower acknowledges the referee and attempts to gain sympathy from fans (while simultaneously *"playing"* the referee).

VARIATIONS: A player will hold the ball and wipe it with their shirt to give the impression the ball is slippery. A player may also wipe their *"wet, sweaty"* hands to further delay the restart.

BENEFIT/CONSEQUENCES: Beware the referee!

If this happens excessively, the referee may caution the time-waster.

TW8 CORNER FLAG MAGNET

TW8 DARK ART DESCRIPTION: Taking the ball to the corner flag is a good time-wasting technique. Due to the shape of the football pitch, approaching the corner areas are the optimal dead-end places to keep possession and run down the clock. For teams who want to waste time, they take the ball to the corners that are furthest away from their own goal. The advantage is that should their team's attacking player break through the defenders, they can suddenly attack the goal to score. Eventually, if the ball goes out of play, it will either be a goal kick, corner kick or a throw-in. If the restart is for the attacking team, it allows them to repeat this time-wasting tactic. But no matter who wins the restart, the objective of running down the clock is achieved.

VARIATIONS: Players can take the ball to the corner flags in their own defensive half. This way, more teammates can help crowd around the corner flag and frustrate opponents.

BENEFIT/CONSEQUENCES: Beware time-wasters!
Some frustrated players have even taken to using the corner flag as a weapon to vent their anger at opposing players for time-wasting. Or opponents will impatiently chop down the player who is wasting time.

ONLINE SEARCH: *"David Luis corner flag"*

In this example, Chelsea defender David Luis wastes time and successfully tricks Manchester United's Rafael da Silva into kicking him. The United player's overreaction is a bonus for the team wasting time because the referee uses up more precious time to send off the player.[15]

TW9 STOP-AND-THINK KICK

TW9 DARK ART DESCRIPTION: At a restart (i.e. free kick, goal kick, corner kick), a player will make a run up to put the ball in play and then suddenly stop, pretending he has no options for finding his teammates. The player can raise his hands, palms up, in a gesture to indicate difficulty in putting the ball into play because he has no options.

VARIATIONS: This "stop-and-think" action can also be done at throw-ins.

The player may also pause and pretend to adjust his kit, socks, pads and even bootlaces. Or, a player's teammate on the pitch can stoop down and tie their bootlaces, thus giving another excuse to delay putting the ball in play (i.e. *"Hey ref, my teammate's not ready!"*).

BENEFIT/CONSEQUENCES: There is no set time limit on restarting play in the rulebook. So if a player's teammates are not ready because they are tying up their bootlaces or if a player has no options to pass the ball, it can look like they have the permission of the spectators to pause and consider their options. This might be enough to persuade the referee not to caution for unsporting behaviour (i.e. time-wasting).

TW10 STRETCHER FETCHER

TW10 DARK ART DESCRIPTION: Toward the end of a match, a player will fake an injury to run down the clock. The player will seek help from their medical staff. Eventually they make out that it is a serious injury, so the referee has no choice but to call on a stretcher. Since the player has to leave the field, he may as well make a whole song-and-dance about it. When the stretcher-bearers arrive, much fuss will be made about the stretcher, its safety straps, which way to lie down, and which direction to head off the pitch. This dark art is executed only when the team has a commanding lead whereby it is highly unlikely in the final minutes of the match that they will concede a few goals and lose.

VARIATIONS: Once the stretcher-bearers arrive, the *"injured"* player will insist on walking off the pitch himself. This is partly because it is a fake injury and partly because it is a *"macho"* thing in football, where a male player chooses to project himself as *"manning up"* and thus walks off slowly rather than be carried quickly off the pitch. A better variation is to use the goalkeeper to fake an injury as in the **TW19 Goalie Timeout** trick, since this avoids the team putting themselves at a numerical disadvantage.

BENEFIT/CONSEQUENCES: Once off the pitch and play has restarted, the player will suddenly get up and appear better and eager to get back on the pitch (because the team is now a player down). They yell at the referee for permission to return to the field of play. However, the referee can sometimes delay the player's return, or even issue a yellow card for obvious unsporting behaviour such as showing *"a lack of respect for the game"*.

ONLINE SEARCH: *"best soccer fake injuries"*.

GOALKEEPER TIME-WASTING

A look at the history of rule changes shows goalkeepers are the biggest time-wasters in the game. FIFA's article: *"Goalkeepers are not above the Law"* describes how their antics has led to many rule amendments over the decades.[16]

In the early days of the game, goalkeepers were allowed to handle the ball with no time limitations. It was simply assumed that goalkeepers would release the ball back into play at a reasonable time without delay. However, without time limitations, it became apparent goalkeepers held on to the ball for as long as they liked, and they also moved around the penalty area as much as they liked, so long as they bounced or juggled the ball as they moved. It was up to opposition players to snatch or swipe the ball away from the goalkeeper in a fair and sporting manner, which is impossible to do unless the keeper had *"butterfingers"*. Increasingly, opponents became frustrated with goalkeepers keeping possession for too long and would often charge at them as tensions built up, so the rules had to be changed. This was done both to protect goalkeepers as well as to minimise their time-wasting antics.

In the 1960s, the four-step rule was introduced in an attempt to reduce the number of unfair challenges on goalkeepers and to help speed up the game. Keepers were supposed to just take four steps and then release the ball. However, keepers soon exploited the rules and interpreted this to mean they could handle the ball, take one or two steps away from opponents and then release it on the ground to dribble somewhere else in the penalty area and still technically have two or three more steps when they picked up the ball again.

This led to a further rule change that stated if the goalkeeper had the ball in his hand and released it on the ground, he would not be able to handle the ball again unless another player played it. So keepers bent the rules by simply throwing the ball to a nearby teammate standing inside the penalty area, who would just kick it back to the keeper, who could then pick up the ball again. This process was repeated again and again to run down the clock.

Another amendment meant that goalkeepers releasing the ball from their possession needed the ball to be played outside the penalty area before the keeper could handle the ball again. It was meant to make it riskier for goalkeepers to make short passes to their defenders because there was a chance of the ball being intercepted by opposition players positioned outside the penalty area.

Goalkeepers quickly developed more time-wasting tactics. Whenever a ball was shot or crossed into the penalty area, instead of catching the ball, keepers started deliberately parrying the ball (i.e. using their hands to pat the ball down to their feet) when they could so easily have held onto the ball with their hands. Parrying enabled keepers to dribble the ball to the edge of their penalty area before picking it up. In effect, goalkeepers were handling the ball twice without first releasing the ball from their possession. Again, the rules were changed to prevent goalkeepers from deliberately parrying and then handling the ball again.

However, the biggest negative tactic involving goalkeepers was the fact that defenders and teammates, even from the halfway line, could deliberately pass back the ball to the goalkeeper who would then handle it, and still take his time in using up his four steps. This became an easy time-wasting tactic, and many televised games before 1992 were boring, monotonous, uninspiring matches where as soon as a team took the lead, they would simply keep possession and repeatedly pass the ball safely back to their unmarked goalkeeper.

Thus, the back-pass rule was first introduced in 1992 to stop goalkeepers from keeping possession by handling the ball excessively and unfairly. Incredibly, there was still no time limit imposed on the goalkeeper when handling the ball. The back-pass rule only meant that if a ball was deliberately kicked by a teammate back to the goalkeeper, then the goalkeeper would not be able to handle the ball, otherwise an indirect free kick would be awarded.

In 1997, the back-pass rule was extended to include prohibiting goalkeepers from handling the ball directly from a throw-in. Players had worked out that deliberately throwing the ball back to their goalkeepers was technically different to kicking the ball back, and hence this proved to be a loophole around the 1992 rule change. This amendment made defending teams play the ball further upfield, rather than risk the relatively poorer footwork of their goalkeepers who would otherwise be closed down and pressured by the opposition.

Finally in 1998, the six-second rule was introduced, which limited goalkeepers to keeping hold of the ball for no more than six seconds. This was initially combined with the four-step rule, but due to complaints that the two rules together were too restrictive, the four-step rule was swiftly abandoned. These days, goalkeepers know they have six seconds from the moment they handle the ball to releasing it from their hands … but this has not prevented them from continuing to try their luck in wasting time!

ONLINE SEARCH: *"football Mignolet six seconds"*.

In this example, the goalkeeper has totally overstayed his welcome, taking 22 seconds to release the ball from his hands.[17] The referee correctly penalized the goalkeeper for his time-wasting antics by awarding an indirect free kick at the place where Liverpool goalkeeper Simon Mignolet was holding the ball for far too long.

The history of the rule changes in relation to goalkeepers wasting time is a perfect example of the ongoing battle between masters of the dark arts and the lawmakers who want to encourage open, constructive, and positive play. It demonstrates how a dark art can creep in and soon develop negatively to affect the game, which in turn forces the game's lawmakers to amend the official written rules, which then is modified by players in what is a continuing *"arms race"* between the game's lawmakers and its practitioners.

The modern example of a new rule change to speed up *the Beautiful Game* is for taking goal kicks. Previously at goal kicks, the ball had to leave the penalty area for it to be in play; now the ball is in play as soon as it is kicked and clearly moves. The ball no longer has to leave the penalty area, which means defenders can no longer deliberately force a retake by stepping inside the penalty area to play the ball. Although IFAB has eliminated this particular dark art (i.e. deliberately forcing one's own retake to waste time), what history has shown is that players, and particularly goalkeepers, will continue developing their dark arts to remain one or two steps ahead of the lawmakers.

Here are a variety of ways goalkeepers continue to run down the clock.

TW11 MYSTERIOUSLY LOOSE LACES

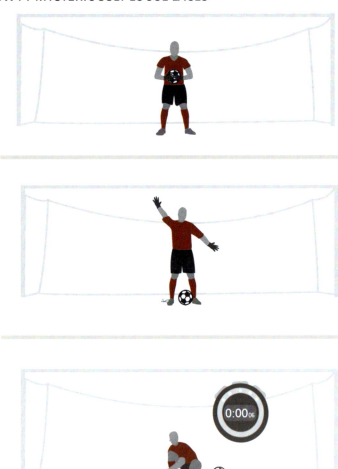

TW11 DARK ART DESCRIPTION: Goalkeepers will usually waste time by claiming their bootlaces are loosened or undone. During a goal kick, a goalkeeper will raise his hand and shout to get the referee's attention. He will then point down to his feet, slowly take his gloves off, and then untie and re-tie their laces. He then

needs to put his gloves back on and reposition the ball on the goal area line to restart. Since the referee is standing far away (usually by the halfway line), the referee cannot possibly see whether the goalkeeper's laces are undone or not.

VARIATIONS: A goalkeeper may ask a teammate to tie up their laces for them, instead of taking off their gloves and then putting them back on again, to give the impression they are *"not really"* wasting time. In fact, they are still running down the clock.

CONSEQUENCES/BENEFIT: It is funny how goalkeepers do not seem to know how to tie up their own laces. Compared with outfield players and even match officials who rarely tie up their laces during a match, goalkeepers do this more frequently. We know this is gamesmanship, and therefore opposition players must understand this is a con too. This tactic can irritate the opposition, and players with lower EQ will begin to complain to the referee, which in turn adds to the time-wasting since the referee will then have to calm down the irate player or players before restarting play.

ONLINE SEARCH: *"goalkeeper wastes time by untying his shoe"*.

In this example, a crafty goalkeeper deliberately unties his own laces and then asks the referee for time to do them up again.

TW12 GOALIE STOP AND DRINK

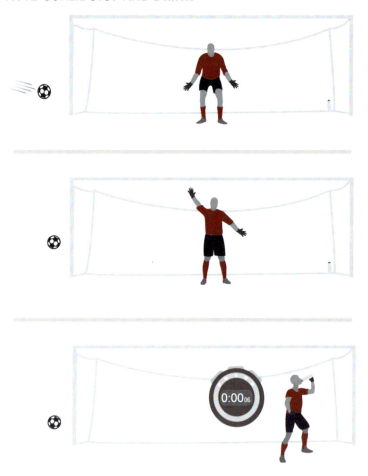

TW12 DARK ART DESCRIPTION: Goalkeepers will usually waste time by taking a swig of water from their drink bottle as soon as the ball goes out of play, instead of focusing on getting the ball back into play. This is an obvious trick because goalkeepers are not the most physically active compared with their outfield teammates, and yet goalkeepers are seen to drink the most water during the

match. Studies show goalkeepers cover less than 1km during a match and walk for about 73% of the match, whereas outfield players and referees easily run between 9km and 12km during a match.[18]

BENEFIT/CONSEQUENCES: Beware time-wasters!

This is obviously a time-wasting tactic, but keepers do this because they think they can appeal to the referees' sense of *"humanity"* in allowing them to quench their thirst, more so on particularly hot sunny days.

ONLINE SEARCH: *"Chinese goalkeeper drinking water misses goal", "German goalkeeper drinking water misses goal".*

Here are examples of goalkeepers being caught unawares. To some observers this is karma since goalkeepers in such situations intentionally planned to waste time and subsequently their time trickery backfired on them.[19]

TW13 GOAL KICK PLACEMENT PUZZLE

TW13 DARK ART DESCRIPTION: When the ball goes out for a goal kick, goalkeepers can take the ball and place it anywhere in the goal area to restart. This represents a distance of over 18 meters (20 yards) from one end of the goal area to the other end—and a total area of 100 sq. m (120 sq. yds)—within which to place the ball. So, if the ball goes out over the goal line on the left side of the goal, goalkeepers are officially entitled to go and place the ball all the way

over on the far right side of the goal, should they wish. Goalkeepers know this and use it to waste time.

BENEFIT/CONSEQUENCES: Since goalkeepers can place the ball where they like in the goal area, they know referees cannot technically caution them.

Unlike with corner kicks, the law does not require the ball placement for goal kicks to be at the nearest location to where the ball went out of play (i.e. the corner kick is taken on the side closest to where the ball went out over the goal line).

Furthermore, because the ball is out of play, there is nothing in the rules that imposes a strict time period for restart. Compare this with a goalkeeper handling the ball during play and the rules imposing a six-second time limit for the goalkeeper to release the ball from his hands.

ONLINE SEARCH: *"fan jumps on keeper"*.

Beware time-wasters! Time-wasting tactics can incur the wrath of fans as well as players. An angry fan runs onto the pitch and hurls himself at the goalkeeper from behind.[20]

TW14 GOAL KICK EAGLE EYES

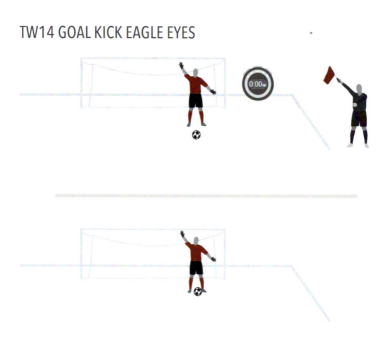

TW14 DARK ART DESCRIPTION: The goalkeeper deliberately places the ball just outside the goal area and relies on the 'eagle eyes' of the assistant referee to spot this infringement and raise his flag. Once the flag is raised, the referee will whistle, and the assistant referee will inform him that the ball is incorrectly placed. The referee will run toward the goalkeeper, shout or make signals about the ball placement. The goalkeeper may also pretend he misunderstands the referee's instructions. Finally the keeper will acknowledge the message with a *"thumbs up"* sign and then proceed to reposition the ball onto the goal area line. All this *"acting"* serves to run down the clock.

VARIATIONS: The goalkeeper will lob the ball with some backspin to the edge of the goal area, giving the impression he has put effort into quickly placing the ball on the goal area line and is ready to restart play. However, chances are the ball will roll beyond the goal area line because the goalkeeper has used trick **DD25 Bogus Backspin Toss.** This means the keeper will then have to walk slowly up to the ball, pick it up and reposition it onto the goal area line, hence using up more precious seconds.

Another variation is that the ball can still be moving as it is kicked, which also relies on the 'eagle eyes' of the match officials. All restarts must begin with the ball stationary.

TW15 GOAL KICK EXTRA BALL

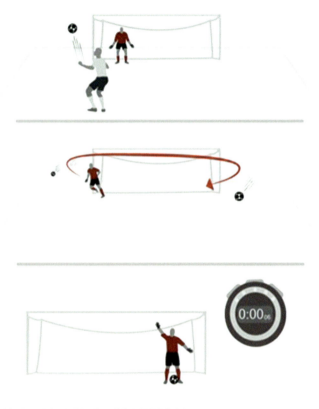

TW15 DARK ART DESCRIPTION: As the ball crosses the goal line and goes out of play, the goalkeeper will signal to the ball boy to throw a spare ball onto the pitch. But the goalkeeper will continue to go out to retrieve the first ball that has gone out of play. When the goalkeeper returns with the original ball, he will drop it down on the pitch, being careful not to return the ball to the ball boy. Instead he will then slowly go and retrieve the other ball from the penalty area and return that one to the ball boy, giving the impression it was the ball boy's fault for throwing the spare ball onto the pitch, which has caused a delay. Finally, the goalkeeper returns to the original ball and repositions it ready for restart.

VARIATIONS: A goalkeeper can also test the pressure of the ball and make a display that it has lost some air. If multiple balls are used, the goalkeeper can signal to the ball boy to throw him another ball to check. By comparing the pressure of the balls, the goalkeeper can run down the clock.

BENEFIT/CONSEQUENCES:

Providing the competition uses multiple balls, this is a good opportunity for goalkeepers (and also players) to exploit ball boys by putting two balls onto the pitch and delaying the restart of play.

TW16 GOAL KICK GO SLOW

TW16 DARK ART DESCRIPTION: As the ball goes out for a goal kick, the goalkeeper will move slowly behind the goal-line, taking the longest way around the goal. Once the keeper has the ball, he will also squeeze and bounce the ball several times,

pretending to test the firmness of the ball. After placing the ball carefully on the goal area line, he walks slowly back to his goalpost for a long run up. He can also use up more time signalling to teammates to move into position before running up to kick the ball.

VARIATIONS: Similar to the **TW9 Stop-And-Think Kick**. Also, after going through all the motions of appearing to take the kick, the goalkeeper then calls on a teammate, who is usually standing outside the penalty area, to take it.

TW17 GOALIE PICKUP DELAY

TW17 DARK ART DESCRIPTION: Goalkeepers will delay handling the ball because they know they have six seconds from the time the ball is in their possession. This happens when an opponent fires in a relatively tame shot or when a teammate uses any part of

the body (except the feet) to knock the ball towards the goalkeeper. To buy time, the goalkeeper will control the ball without using his hands, allowing it to settle near his feet. When an approaching opponent challenges them, they will pick up the ball with their hands. Sometimes, they grab the ball with both hands and flop to the ground, buying an extra couple of seconds before getting back up on their feet to release the ball.

BENEFIT/CONSEQUENCES: This time-wasting tactic goads an opponent to approach and hurry the goalkeeper to pick up the ball. A benefit of this trick is when the opponent overreacts, or if the goalkeeper playacts to an opponents' physical approach. This can result in a red card to the opponent and further delay.

ONLINE SEARCH: *"van Persie foul on goalkeeper"*

In this example, goalkeeper Thomas Sorensen deliberately goads Robin van Persie to commit a brutal foul and receive a red card.

"Goalkeeper tries to time-waste EPIC FAIL".

Beware time-wasters! This goalkeeper tries to be too clever and makes a critical mistake.[21]

> *"I was teasing him a bit. I could see the frustration in his eyes and I used that."*

—Thomas Sorensen on Robin van Persie's red card[22]

TW18 CHEAP TRICK THROW

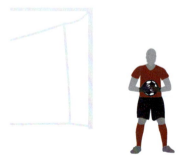

TW18 DARK ART DESCRIPTION: At the highest levels, goalkeepers have no need to leave the surrounds of their goal area to retrieve the ball that has just gone out of play. There are ball boys who do the legwork. However, when running down the clock, there is nothing to stop goalkeepers from wanting to retrieve the ball themselves. They will energetically jump over the advertising hoardings and pretend they are quickly retrieving the ball. When they finally get the ball, they will walk slowly back to the pitch, and perhaps deliberately *"lose"* or *"fumble"* the ball on their way back.

VARIATIONS: A goalkeeper can energetically jump over the advertising hoardings and then pretend to injure himself (see **TW19 Goalie Timeout)**. By asking for medical treatment, this cheap trick helps the goalkeeper run down the clock because the rules allow goalkeepers to receive medical treatment before restarting play.

ONLINE SEARCH: *"Jens Lehman wasting time"*

In this example, goalkeeper Jens Lehmann, when retrieving the ball from beyond the advertising hoardings, *"accidentally"* throws the ball at the back of the advertising hoarding, which bounces back away from the pitch, so he has to retrieve it again.[23]

TW19 GOALIE TIMEOUT

TW19 DARK ART DESCRIPTION: The goalkeeper, having gained possession of the ball or gained a goal kick, will suddenly go to ground and ask for a time out, making sure the ball is first put out of play. Goalkeepers are the only players on the pitch who can ask for treatment on the pitch. All they have to do is express to the referee that they are hurt, and the referee will usually whistle to stop the game, communicate with the goalkeeper, and then ask for the goalkeeper's medical staff to enter the pitch.

BENEFIT/CONSEQUENCES: This dark art delays play and frustrates opponents, especially if the goalkeeper did not have contact with any players leading up to his "injury".

ONLINE SEARCH: *"Senegal goalkeeper fakes injury".*

In the 90th minute, the Senegal goalkeeper deliberately trips over his own feet and feigns injury. This dark art was enough to run down the clock to eliminate opponents Algeria from the 2017 Africa Cup of Nations and for Senegal to retain the top spot in their knockout group.[24]

OTHER TIME-WASTING TACTICS

Substitutes

TW20 SNEAKY SUBS

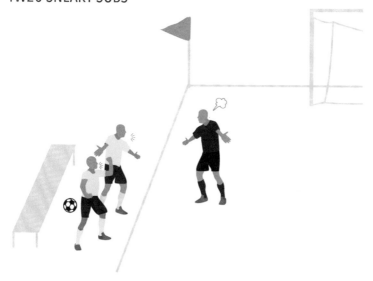

TW20 DARK ART DESCRIPTION: Substitutes warming up on the touchline will take every opportunity to negatively affect their opponents. These sneaky subs will generally just get in the way of opposing players and may even provoke them with sneaky, snide remarks that only they can hear. Tricky subs will also perform the **TW1 False Fetch** ruse on opponents who are quickly trying to retrieve the ball from the side of the pitch to restart play.

VARIATIONS: Substitutes may verbally spar with and provoke an opponent who is about to take a throw-in or corner kick, to make him lose focus. This is trick **DD1 Pushing Buttons: Verbal.**

Also, when ball boys are rushing to get the ball to the home team to help them chase the game, substitutes from the away team may deliberately obstruct ball boys from doing their jobs.

BENEFIT/CONSEQUENCES: Opponents may *"rise to the bait"* and retaliate, thus ensuring the referee will get involved and further delay proceedings. If a player becomes embroiled with an opposing substitute and both get sent off, one team will have one player fewer on the pitch. The sneaky sub has created a numerical advantage for his team.

Coaches

TW21 SUPER-SLOW SUB

TW21 DARK ART DESCRIPTION: A player is substituted near the end of a match, usually in added time. Coaches know match officials usually grant 30 seconds for a substitution, so they will draw

out this process as long as possible. It used to be the canny coach would substitute off a player who he knows will be located on the other side of the pitch far away from the technical area. But because of the modern rule changes, a player who is being substituted must now leave the field at the nearest point on the boundary line (so players who know they are being taken off will try to be more centrally positioned). The centrally located player who is being substituted can then act indecisively, first moving in one direction to leave the pitch and then doubling back by going in the opposite direction. Furthermore, the substituted player can walk slowly, turn around to clap and wave to supporters, and attempt to seek out the referee to shake hands. Referees know this is all show and the main aim is to run down the clock as much as possible.

BENEFIT/CONSEQUENCES: Beware time-wasters!

When deliberately coming off the pitch at slow speed and seeking to shake the hand of the referee, such players may be cautioned for excessive time-wasting. However, the time-waster may also be confronted by opposition players who will try to hurry him off the pitch, perhaps even pushing him and causing a ruckus, which will help run down the clock.

TW22 CRAFTY COACHES

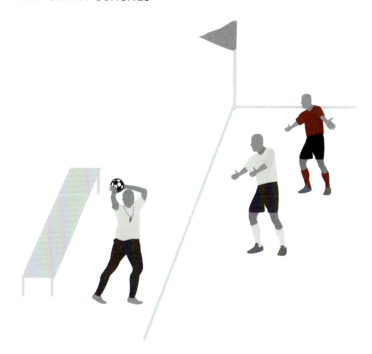

TW22 DARK ART DESCRIPTION: Coaches will keep the ball and prevent an opposition player from taking the throw-in quickly.

BENEFIT/CONSEQUENCES: Since one person is allowed to stand up in the technical area, managers have an opportunity to engage in touchline trickery and to delay proceedings like a throw-in.

EXAMPLES: Manchester City manager Pep Guardiola withheld the ball from Manchester United's Wayne Rooney during the 2016-2017 EPL season.[25]

Chelsea manager José Mourinho withheld the ball from Liverpool's Steven Gerrard in April 2014.[26]

Newcastle manager Alan Pardew performed the **TW1 False Fetch** and then followed this up by headbutting Hull City's David Meyler in March 2014.[27]

ONLINE SEARCH: *"football coach hit by paper plane"*.

Some managers will feign being injured, even when a harmless object like a paper plane lands on them. This is perhaps to demonstrate to their own players how to perform the dark arts!

Ball Boys

TW23 BALL BOY BOP

TW23 DARK ART DESCRIPTION: Ball boys are usually the home side's youth team players and apprentices, and therefore have an inherent bias toward their own team. They know the game well and understand when a team is chasing the game or running down the clock. Ball boys will keep the ball and prevent an opposition player from taking the throw-in, goal kick, or corner kick quickly.

VARIATIONS: Ball boys, who look young and innocent, will use abusive language and gestures against opposition players. If players react negatively, the bonus is when the referee takes disciplinary action against them.

BENEFIT/CONSEQUENCES: The benefit is to get opponents to react, so that they are frustrated and lose focus on chasing the game.

ONLINE SEARCH: *"ball boy time wasting"*.

In this example, a Swansea ball boy holds on to the match ball and refuses to immediately return the ball to Chelsea, the away team. Chelsea's Eden Hazard falls for the trap and consequently is sent off.[28]

We know ball boys help waste time in delaying restarts because conversely, they can also help teams speed up on restarts.

ONLINE SEARCH *"Liverpool quick thinking ball boy"*.

In this example, a ball boy from Liverpool *"assisted"* in his home team's win against Barcelona in the Champions League by rapidly releasing the ball to enable a quick corner kick, which led to Liverpool's decisive goal.

Fans

TW24 FREAKY FANS

TW24 DARK ART DESCRIPTION: The aim is for fans to goad players to react, so consequently they will be disciplined. Sometimes fans will run onto the pitch to confront players. If a player reacts using violent conduct, the player leaves the referee with no choice but to send them off.

VARIATIONS: The most infamous Freaky Fan incident is Matthew Simmons, a Crystal Palace fan, who managed to use the **DD1 Pushing Buttons: Verbal** ploy to provoke an already-dismissed Eric Cantona of Manchester United to launch himself, double-footed, into the loud-mouthed supporter.[29] Although already sent off, Cantona received a lengthy ban for this physical outburst against a spectator. He was handed a 9-month ban plus 120 hours community service. The freaky fan's behaviour caused huge drama and significantly delayed the restart of the match.

BENEFIT/CONSEQUENCES: Players should remain calm, professional, and not react to pitch invaders. They should allow the stewards to deal with the situation. Players who do not heed this advice and take matters into their own hands will likely get sent off for violent conduct and face additional disciplinary action.

ONLINE SEARCH: *"Eric Cantona kung-fu kick"*; *"Crazy Football Fights".*

ONLINE SEARCH: *"pitch invaders"* and *"funniest and most violent pitch invaders".*

TW25 PELTING PLAYERS

TW25 DARK ART DESCRIPTION: Players taking corners will be put under intense pressure when surrounded by opposition fans. They will be blasted with shocking insults and other verbal abuse, and may also be bombarded with physical objects. The missiles and projectiles include water bottles, coins, keys, and cigarette lighters. These are just some of the *"nicer"* items that fans will throw at players to delay them from taking the corner kick.

VARIATIONS: In Spain, they haul on pig or cow heads. In Turkey, they launch flares and firecrackers. In Denmark, they lob dead rats.

ONLINE SEARCH: *"football fans pig head"*; *"football fans fireworks"*; *"football fans throw dead rats"*.

BENEFIT/CONSEQUENCES: If a player reacts or complains to the referee, this only serves to help run down the clock. A huge benefit for time-wasters is when a referee has no choice but to temporarily suspend the match. Following the time out, players will not be at the same adrenaline-fuelled level, and therefore the remaining match time will fizzle out like a damp squib.

SUMMARY OF TIME-WASTING TACTICS

There are plenty of online videos demonstrating how players run down the clock.

ONLINE SEARCH: *"football how to waste time"; "football players wasting time"; "footballer wasting time"; "funny time waster moments in football".*

2 DEVILISH DECEPTIONS

Another dark arts category is *"getting away with murder"*. Well not literally, obviously, but rather players doing something underhanded that will either put their opponents in a bad light or place themselves as innocent victims, or both. Deception ploys against opponents, opposition coaches and match officials are all executed to gain an unfair advantage and ultimately to win.

Marco Materazzi, the former Italy defender and a favourite player of Mourinho, knows this only too well. Nicknamed *"the Butcher"*, he practically decided, or at least played a significant role in, the outcome of the 2006 World Cup Final by goading France star Zinedine Zidane to overreact with violence.

Materazzi, a master of the dark arts, outplayed, outfought, and outwitted the majestically skilful Zidane and became the ultimate winner that season in lifting the World Cup (having also won Serie A and the Coppa Italia with Inter Milan).

To this day Zidane remains angered by Materazzi's verbal provocation, which led to his infamous headbutt on Materazzi and dismissal in his last-ever match as a professional player. He publicly said he would rather die than apologise to Materazzi for violently headbutting him on the pitch.[30]

"If I say sorry, I would also be admitting that what he [Materazzi] himself did was normal. And for me it was not normal. Things happen on the pitch. More than once they insulted my mother and I never responded. But there [I hit him]. But my mother was ill. She was in hospital. This people did not know. I apologise to football, to the fans, to the team ... But to him [Materazzi] I cannot. Never, never ... it would be to dishonour me ... I'd rather die. There are evil people. And I don't even want to hear those guys speak."

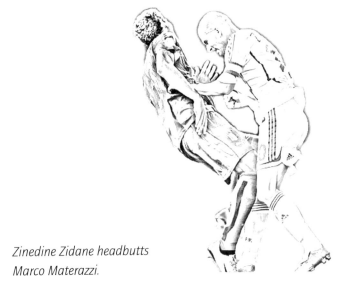

Zinedine Zidane headbutts Marco Materazzi.

Zidane claimed that verbal abuse to him *"was not normal"*. However, clever players know how to push their opponents' buttons, like making irritating or intimidating remarks, and inflicting psychological abuse. Experienced players like *"the Butcher"* who want a competitive edge over their opponents will make the **DD1 Pushing Buttons: Verbal** ruse a typical part of their game.

These devilish deceptions and dirty tricks reveal the hypocrisy and unsporting behaviour that exist in football, especially at the highest, competitive levels. Players pretend to be all nice and friendly to one another, but once the whistle sounds, there are no more pleasantries. At both the individual and team level, those who limit their play to talent, flair, and honesty (the positive "light side") will be left behind by those who cleverly include knowledge of the dark arts in their repertoire.

This second section lists 30 crafty tricks related to the dark arts of conning, deceiving, and exploiting opponents and match officials.

ABUSIVE DARK ARTS

DD1 PUSHING BUTTONS: VERBAL

DD1 DARK ART DESCRIPTION: Players will do anything to irritate and get a reaction from opposition players, usually by trash talking or teasing. It's most obvious when defenders and attackers go at it, but it occurs all over the pitch whenever players frequently tussle against each other. Players know whether certain opponents have a short fuse or are *"precious"* about being teased. Even personal stories splashed by the media will be used to provoke and get a reaction from opposition players.

VARIATIONS: Bizarre Banter; Psychological Intimidation; Verbal Abuse (which extends to racist, religious, sexist and other discriminatory remarks)

BENEFIT/CONSEQUENCES: If a team has a star player who cannot be touched on footballing terms (i.e. skill versus skill), then opponents using this dark art of verbal abuse may elicit the necessary negative reaction. Zidane's violent overreaction against Materazzi's constant stream of verbal abuse is the ultimate example.[30]

PREVENTION: Although difficult in this day and age, keeping your personal life private is really the best deterrent because it reduces the amount of *"ammunition"* your enemies and opponents can use against you.

ONLINE SEARCH: *"football chats"* and *"football hidden chats"*.

DD2 PUSHING BUTTONS: HANDS

DD2 DARK ART DESCRIPTION: A *"wet willy"* is a damp, cold object (usually a sweat- or saliva-moistened finger) that is inserted in an unsuspecting opponent's ear, with a twisting motion to ensure the victim knows he's being aggravated and violated.

A "wet willy"

VARIATIONS: Hands Around Neck; Hands on Face

BENEFIT/CONSEQUENCES: The wet willy prank, and other unnecessary hand actions, can elicit the necessary negative reaction from an opponent.

ONLINE SEARCH: *"football wet willy"*.

In this dark art example, Plymouth player Sonny Bradley wiped his finger under the armpit of Liverpool's Emre Can before poking his finger in his opponent's ear during a 2017 FA Cup tie between the two sides.

Can protested to the referee, but since the match official did not see it, there is little that can be done. To the referee, Bradley appears innocent, and Can appears to be whinging about something just to get a favourable decision.[31]

DD3 PUSHING BUTTONS: OTHER BODY PARTS

DD3 DARK ART DESCRIPTION: When players get into each other's personal space, things can get unpleasant. Some players will resort to grabbing genitals (Gonad Grab), just to provoke a reaction from their opponents.

The gonad grab

VARIATIONS: Nipple Squeeze; Eye Gouge; Hair Pull; Rabbit Punch; Knee to Back; Finger in Butt (or *"Oil Check"*)

BENEFIT/CONSEQUENCES: Players know a *"below the belt"* action or a grab at a vulnerable body part can elicit the necessary negative reaction from an opponent. Chile's Gonzalo Jara gave an *"oil check"* to Uruguay's Edison Cavani. The victim retaliated by striking his unsporting opponent in the face and was sent off. Chile and Jara went on to beat Uruguay, and ultimately triumphed at the 2015 Copa America.[32]

ONLINE SEARCH: *"Vinnie Jones Paul Gascoigne"; "Mourinho eye gouge"; "Jara finger Cavani"*

DD4 PUSHING BUTTONS: SPITTING AND BITING

DD4 DARK ART DESCRIPTION: In many countries and cultures, spitting and biting are considered disgusting, despicable, and downright dirty, in the hygienic sense, which is why it is socially unacceptable.

Biting and spitting at an opponent, match official, spectator, or anyone is its own category of red card offence, which is distinct from violent conduct defined as headbutting, kicking, punching, and striking someone with brutality.

However, biting clearly violates the victim's body. According to Orin Starn, professor of Cultural Anthropology and History at Duke University in the United States:[33] *"Biting has broken the boundary of the body, which in western culture is a taboo."*

VARIATIONS: Physical Intimidation; Physical Challenges;

Former Arsenal and Manchester City forward Emmanuel Adebayor had this to say about Manchester United defenders Rio Ferdinand

and Nemanja Vidic, whom he faced numerous times in the English Premier League:[34]

*"Rio insulted everyone on the pitch. He is proper psycho! But Vidic was the tough man, the nastiest, like running into a rock. He could block a striker with a single finger. He walks on you, he says sorry, he kicks you, he says sorry. **He shouts at you and makes a little bit of spit come out.** This guy was ready to kill."*

BENEFIT/CONSEQUENCES: These dark arts can disgust and inflame opponents enough to elicit the necessary negative reaction, which if seen by match officials will result in expulsion for violent conduct.

ONLINE SEARCH: *"football Luis Suarez bite"*

Luis Suarez has a history of biting his opponents, having been disciplined three times in his career. His most infamous incident was at the 2014 World Cup between Uruguay and Italy.

However, following the fallout, no one questioned whether Giorgio Chiellini provoked Suarez in the first place. Looking at Italy's own masters of the dark arts, it will come as little surprise to discover that Chiellini was trying to provoke Suarez throughout the match (**DD1 Pushing Buttons: Verbal**) and trying to intimidate him (**DD5 Calculated Intimidation**).

DD5 CALCULATED INTIMIDATION

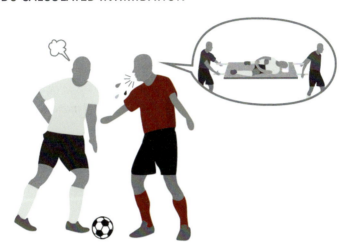

DD5 DARK ART DESCRIPTION: Players knowingly intimidate opponents, especially in the opening minutes of a match. They will also deliberately target opponents who have just returned from injury or who are known to be injury prone. Knowing that referees are usually lenient at the beginning of the match, a calculated early foul to physically hurt an opponent may be enough to elicit some retaliation from the opponent.

VARIATIONS: Players are sometimes bold enough to tackle an opponent from behind, knowing full well that referees will be under pressure not to send them off. Particularly if the player's teammates help with distraction tricks, by surrounding and hounding the referee (see **DD26 Rile the Referee**). In return for a yellow card for the player's cowardly act, the opponent is affected both physically and psychologically for the remainder of the match.

BENEFIT/CONSEQUENCES: Opponents may take matters into their own hands and retaliate with violent conduct, which may be seen by the match officials.

RECKLESS DARK ARTS

"It's a part of Giorgio Chiellini's game — that aggression, the dark arts. He's a wily old character. When you're a defender you have to let the forward know what you're about. Without getting a yellow card or being too stupid, let him know that at some point you're going to hurt him so he's weary and that's what these Italians are known for."

—Rio Ferdinand, former Manchester United and England defender[35]

DD6 SECRET STAMPER

DD6 DARK ART DESCRIPTION: To intentionally stand or stamp on an opponent's foot, and to make it look accidental or as if it didn't happen at all. This can happen whenever players are standing in each other's personal space (e.g. jostling at corner kicks and set pieces, and when players are on the ground surrounded by opponents).

VARIATIONS: Stand or stamp on other part of opponent's body, like the leg, hand, or head.[36, 37]

BENEFIT/CONSEQUENCES: Players know this sneaky stamp can elicit the necessary negative reaction from an opponent because it can cause a lot of pain. The sly stamp is easy for match officials to miss, but the often very loud reaction is easier to see and can put the victim in trouble rather than the initial troublemaker.

Manchester United and Argentina defender Marcos Rojo admitted to deliberately kicking and stamping on his opponents like Alexis Sanchez. There is a photograph of Rojo stamping on Sanchez's ankle when they played on opposing sides.[38]

ONLINE SEARCH: *"Pepe stamps on Messi"*; *"Diego Costa stamp"*; *"Balotelli stamp"*; *"Eric Lamela and Cesc Fabregas"*.

DD7 BOOT OVER THE TOP (BOTT)

DD7 DARK ART DESCRIPTION: When two opposing players come together in a 50-50 challenge for the ball, one player will deliberately go over the top of the ball with his foot. The malicious intent is to make contact with the onrushing opponent and to cause injury, while making it appear accidental.

BENEFIT/CONSEQUENCES: During the 2002 world cup match between Brazil and England, Ronaldinho was sent off for BOTT (i.e. for being a *"bottler"* in a 50-50 challenge). The BOTT is a cowardly and unsporting act. The referee was not fooled by this dark art, but the victim England defender Danny Mills remains duped to this day, saying it was not a red card and only a booking. Mills revealed what happened from his perspective in a frank radio interview in 2016.[39, 40]

ONLINE SEARCH: *"Ronaldinho vs England WC 2002".*

DD8 LEAVE A BIT ON (LABO)

DD8 DARK ART DESCRIPTION: Football is a contact sport, and players use this to their advantage knowing that everyone receives knocks, knees, and kicks to their bodies. When a player is not quick enough to block or stop an opponent from clearing or crossing the ball, he will still *"leave a bit on"*. That is, a player will ensure that

he makes contact with the opponent's foot or lower leg during the opponent's follow-through action of kicking the ball.

VARIATIONS: Intimidation (**DD5 Calculated Intimidation**); Physical Challenges such as pulling, pushing or holding on to opponents (e.g. *"Ramos on Salah"*)

BENEFIT/CONSEQUENCES: An intentional foul to intimidate and physically hurt an opponent may be enough to elicit some retaliation from the opponent.

> *"It used to be that central defenders would rattle the centre forward early on, put a bit more into the challenge than you need to. With Diego Costa [at Chelsea] it's the reverse – he wants to leave a little bit on the centre half."*

—Martin Keown, former Arsenal and England defender[41]

A riled Deli Ali retaliates with brutality, resulting in a red card.

> *"He had taken a hard tackle immediately beforehand but that was no justification for the lunge that appeared to bend Brecht Dejaegere's shin. The bone so easily could have snapped."*

—Harry Redknapp, former Tottenham Hotspur manager[42]

DD9 NAUGHTY NUDGE

DD9 DARK ART DESCRIPTION: ALWAYS nudge or push a player. The Naughty Nudge can occur anywhere on the pitch where players are crowding each other. For instance, if an incoming attacker and goalkeeper run toward each other to challenge for the ball, the nearest defender who cannot fairly challenge the attacker will attempt to nudge the attacker to make him lose balance and appear to foul the goalkeeper.

ONLINE SEARCH: *"Lens PSG 3 red cards".*

Here are three examples of players pushing, which the match referee consistently and correctly penalized in a French Ligue 1 game between Lens and Paris Saint Germain.

VARIATIONS: Tricky Tug; Devious Drag; Sly Shirt Pull

The Naughty Nudge can also be used at set pieces to put players in an offside position. At a Manchester United set piece, Liverpool's Sadio Mane pushed Romelu Lukaku forward as the free kick was taken, and the ball entered the Liverpool goal. However, Lukaku had attempted to play the ball from an offside position and the Manchester United goal was disallowed for offside.

ONLINE SEARCH: *"Liverpool Mane pushing Lukaka offside"*.

BENEFIT/CONSEQUENCES: When players are in close proximity, it is difficult for match officials to see sneaky pushes. Wayne Rooney admits to learning how to use the Naughty Nudge to help him win headers:[43]

> *"I didn't score many headers but trained with Mike Phelan, worked on it for about two or three months and then I scored one and they just kept coming. I'm not the tallest but what he worked on was my timing, getting across defenders, giving the defender a nudge before you jump."*

ONLINE SEARCH: *"football Jamie Vardy red card Stoke"*.

This example saw a diverse range of opinions that either agreed or disagreed that the challenge deserved a red card. However, what was abundantly clear is that there was a Naughty Nudge.

> *"People are trying to say he [Leicester player Jamie Vardy] was pushed and that is why he jumped in with two feet off the ground."*

—Mark Hughes, manager of Stoke[44]

DD10 FLATTEN THE OPPONENT

DD10 DARK ART DESCRIPTION: Players will sometimes seek to injure, intimidate, and flatten an opponent. Goalkeepers appear to do this more often because they assume they receive more protection from referees than outfield players. They know they are the last line of defence so when an attacker breaks through on goal,

goalkeepers have a decision to make: *"whether or not to clatter into the opponent".* Goalkeepers who deliberately take out opponents will plead innocent, but the unfair challenge serves to make opponents *"think twice"* before entering into any challenge with the goalkeeper.

VARIATIONS: When catching the ball, goalkeepers will raise one foot, studs up, toward any nearby opponent. Goalkeepers and other players incorrectly assume this is allowed, but the rules clearly state this is an infringement if an opponent is nearby (it is an offence if a player *"kicks or attempts to kick"* an opponent).

ONLINE SEARCH: *"Schumacher Battiston".*

In this infamous example at the 1982 World Cup, West German goalkeeper Harald Schumacher deliberately makes a sickening challenge on France player Patrick Battiston.

Battiston was flattened, lost consciousness, cracked a vertebra, lost some teeth, and was stretchered off. Schumacher received no punishment for his dark art and West Germany went on to win that semi-final match.[45]

ONLINE SEARCH: *"worst goalkeeper tackles".*

DD11 CLUMSY TACTICAL FOUL

DD11 DARK ART DESCRIPTION: The clumsy tactical foul is sly, sneaky, and shrewd. It occurs when the opposition threatens a fast breakaway or counterattack, usually near the halfway line when the attacking team has just lost possession in the final third. The foul impedes an opponent and the guilty player appears to be clumsy so that referees are sometimes fooled into not giving further sanction other than a simple free kick.[46]

VARIATIONS: Also called *"play-breaking tackles"* or sometimes the *"Makelele Foul"*.[47]

ONLINE SEARCH: *"Guardiola five second rule"*.

With the five-second rule made popular by Pep Guardiola, a team must regain possession of the ball within five seconds of losing possession otherwise they should commit a **Clumsy Tactical Foul**.

DD12 COUNTERATTACK DISRUPTOR

DD12 DARK ART DESCRIPTION: Coaches know that an *"outside agent"* can disrupt play. So, coaches have been known to throw another ball onto the pitch to prevent a quick breakaway by the opposing team.

VARIATIONS: Coaches will step onto the pitch with the intention of stopping, tripping, or intimidating an opposition player who is on the counterattack.

BENEFIT/CONSEQUENCES: Referees will temporarily stop play if an outside agent like a dog, ferret, pitch invader, or another ball enters the pitch and interferes with play. If this happens during a counterattack, the defending team will benefit, either by good fortune or by forced circumstances, from the disruption.[48]

ONLINE SEARCH: *"Diego Simeone threw second ball".*

DD13 TUNNEL TAUNTER

DD13 DARK ART DESCRIPTION: The tunnel area of a stadium is the common corridor where opposing teams come together, either on their way out to the pitch or on their way back to their changing rooms. Heated clashes can occur here, and some players and coaches exploit this situation.

BENEFIT/CONSEQUENCES: Tunnel confrontations can occur just before kick-off. In this example, two rival captains have a tense standoff in the tunnel.[49] Players beware! The laws permit referees to caution and send off players who misbehave in the tunnel area, even before the match has officially started.

ONLINE SEARCH: *"Roy Keane and Patrick Vieira fight in tunnel"; "Warnock".*

In the 2005 documentary about seasoned manager Neil Warnock, the referee sends off Millwall defender Kevin Muscat and Sheffield United goalkeeper Paddy Kenny for fighting in the tunnel at halftime.

> *"You know what Muscat's like. He wants to get a response. Muscat is (beep) sly, he does it when nobody's looking. He wants somebody to give him an elbow and get sent off."*

—Neil Warnock, manager, Sheffield United

Even better, if a substitute can get an opponent sent off, this will lead to a numerical advantage on the pitch. In this example, during half time Barcelona reserve goalkeeper José Pinto deliberately clashes with his *El Clasico* opponents in the hope of getting some of them cautioned or sent off. However, in this instance Pinto only managed to get himself sent off.[50]

DD14 FORCED FAKE FOUL

DD14 DARK ART DESCRIPTION: A player, standing behind an opponent, craftily grabs his opponent's arm and uses it to strike himself in the face. The player then falls to ground, and the referee whistles for a free kick against the opponent.

VARIATIONS: A player jumps up for the ball together with an opponent. As the player comes down, he will shout loudly and hold his face as if the opponent's elbow has hit him.

BENEFIT/CONSEQUENCES: Apart from gaining a free kick, if the referee deems the *"foul"* to be reckless enough then a bonus would be to see the opponent being issued with a yellow or red card.[51]

ONLINE SEARCH: *"best soccer fake of all times"*; *"best soccer fake injuries"*.

DD15 NUTTY BUTTY

DD15 DARK ART DESCRIPTION: A player attempts to get an opponent sent off by pretending to be hit in the face. Two opposing players confront each other and put their heads together in a macho faceoff. Suddenly one of them will fling themselves backward, as if they had been headbutted with force, and fall to the ground. This

action is usually enough to get the opponent sent off, particularly if the player continues to writhe in agony and hold his face while sprawled on the ground.[52]

VARIATIONS: A player stamps on an opponent and then suddenly recoils as if his opponent has hit him in the face. In this example, Burnley's Joey Barton first stamps (**DD6 Secret Stamper**) on his opponent Matt Rhead of Lincoln City, and then faked a head injury to get his rival in trouble.[53]

BENEFIT/CONSEQUENCES: It is relatively easy to trick referees into giving red cards because during a faceoff when two heads are close together, a sudden recoil gives the appearance of being on the receiving end of a headbutt. The benefit is the referee is forced to take disciplinary action, which is almost always a red card.

DD16 PHANTOM FOUL

DD16 DARK ART DESCRIPTION: A player will fake a foul in an attempt to get his opponent in trouble, or to get himself out of trouble.

VARIATIONS: When two players come together while chasing the ball, one player may scream and put his hands up to his face to claim he has been struck in the face by his opponent's flailing hand or arm. Sometimes the playacting can be so good that the referee may be duped into giving a yellow or red card to the innocent opponent.

BENEFIT/CONSEQUENCES: If a player loses possession of the ball or fails to win a 50-50 challenge, he may try to gain something *"lucky"* by faking a foul and relying on the sympathy of the referee or the opposition players to stop the game.

ONLINE SEARCH: *"Pepe simulation"*.

Pepe is a master of this dark art art.[54]

DD17 SHAM SIMULATION

DD17 DARK ART DESCRIPTION: A player dives to gain a penalty or a free kick. This is different from the **DD16 Phantom Foul** ruse in that this dark art's main aim is to win an advantageous restart (rather than to seek punishment on an individual opponent).

VARIATION: A sneaky player can also *"trawl"* for a foul. For instance, when an attacker and an onrushing goalkeeper challenge for the ball, the attacker will allow the goalkeeper to slide into him (even though the attacker could so easily *"jump"* out of the way), in the hope of conning the referee to award a penalty.

Many examples of diving (or simulation, to use proper terminology) can be found online. Ashley Young of Manchester United is just one player who has earned a reputation for simulation.

> *"I think he's an absolute disgrace. If he's a Manchester United player then I'm a Chinaman. That shouldn't be accepted at Man United."*

—Roy Keane, former captain, Manchester United, talking about Ashley Young's obvious dive to win a penalty.[55]

Note: Pundit Roy Keane's comments show that racist remarks are still common in and around the game. This should not be accepted anywhere. Kick racism out of the game!

ONLINE SEARCH: *"Ashley Young diving"*.

DD18 RHYTHM BREAKER

DD18 DARK ART DESCRIPTION: During play, a player will fake an injury for no apparent reason, and even with no opponent nearby. The aim is to get the game stopped, either by a sympathetic opponent or by the referee. This usually occurs when the opposition is playing well, so the intent here is to stop and spoil their rhythm, concentration, and adrenalin levels.

VARIATIONS: A player will go near the technical area, and the coach or medical staff will yell at the referee to stop play so that their player can receive immediate medical attention.

ONLINE SEARCH: *"tika taka football"; "rhythmic passing".*

These teams possessed fluid passing, which was hard for opponents to break up (Pep Guardiola's Barcelona champions from 2008 to 2012, and Spain's 2010 and Germany's 2014 World Cup winning teams). Opponents become increasingly frustrated when they fail to win possession of the ball for long periods, so trying to break up their opponent's rhythm is a dark arts tactic.

Another way to *"take the sting out"* of eager opposition who suddenly have momentum in a match is to gain possession and just play the ball back to the defensive line.[56]

DD19 HANDY HANDBALL

DD19 DARK ART DESCRIPTION: When a ball is at chest height, it can be difficult to control. A player may sometimes use their hand to stop the ball, while making sure to give the impression that they used their chest to bring the flight of the ball under their control. The hand (defined as the exposed arm when wearing a

sleeveless shirt) is the only part of the body that cannot play the ball, but sneaky players will attempt to do so if they can.

VARIATIONS: A player uses his hand to prevent a goal, while claiming that the ball hit his chest or back.

BENEFIT/CONSEQUENCES: Match officials have been deceived by these devious sleight of hand tricks, most notably France player Thierry Henry's handball against Ireland that led to a goal in the 2006 World Cup qualifying game.

ONLINE SEARCH: *"Thierry Henry handball vs Ireland"*.

But the most famous dishonest handball is Diego Maradona's *"Hand of God"* goal against England at the 1986 World Cup. Maradona also admitted to a second *"Hand of God"*, but 27 years after it happened.[57, 58] At the 1990 World Cup while defending his own goal at a corner against the Soviet Union, Maradona said he used his hand to stop the ball from flying towards his goal. However, when he was interviewed after the match in 1990, he shrewdly said:

> *"The ball hit me. I made a gesture of raising my arm. I don't know if it would have been a goal."*

DD20 MY MATE'S DOWN

DD20 DARK ART DESCRIPTION: Players can use their injured teammates as a decoy to gain the attention of opponents. As soon as an opponent is focused on their injured teammate, a player can exploit the situation and advance towards the opponent's goal.

BENEFIT/CONSEQUENCES: Making a chump out of opponents and scoring a goal is a huge benefit but beware repercussions.

ONLINE SEARCH: *"Joel Veltman unsporting"*.

In this example in the Eredivisie, Ajax centre back Joel Veltman demonstrated unsporting behaviour in a league clash with Sparta Rotterdam. He exploited opposition goodwill to create an attacking opportunity.[59]

DD21 GRASS CUTTER

DD21 DARK ART DESCRIPTION: Prior to a penalty kick, a devious goalkeeper (or a teammate) loosens the turf area next to the penalty mark. This is done by distracting the referee and making sure everyone is looking around, either towards the goal or technical area, rather than down at their feet.[60]

BENEFIT/CONSEQUENCES: Loosened turf increases the chances that the penalty taker will slip because their landing foot becomes unstable. Hence, they may miskick the ball or even fall over.

ONLINE SEARCH: *"Goalkeeper dirty trick penalty".*

DD22 THIRSTY TRICKSTER

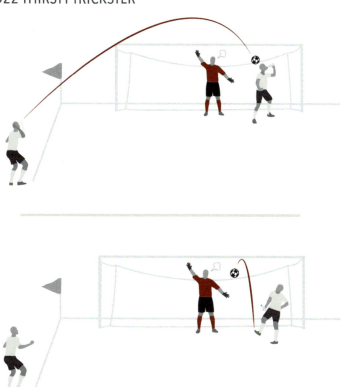

DD22 DARK ART DESCRIPTION: Prior to a throw-in, an attacking player can claim to be thirsty and ask the opposing goalkeeper to give him a drink. At restart, the attacking player conveniently remains near the opponent's goal area and can benefit from this position without being called offside. This clever and cunning trick is attributed to Brazilian Ronaldinho during a league match between Atletico Mineiro and Sao Paulo.

BENEFIT/CONSEQUENCES: The offside rule prevents attacking players from *"goal hanging"*, which is lingering around the goal area. However, the offside rule does not apply to throw-ins, so players can use this loophole in the law to push forward upfield.

ONLINE SEARCH: *"Ronaldinho water bottle trick"*.

In Brazil, Atletico Mineiro beat Sao Paulo 2-1 due to Ronaldinho's crafty assist. Prior to his team's throw-in, which was held up by a substitution procedure, Ronaldinho grabbed a drink from the opposition goalkeeper. He therefore remained far upfield and unmarked ready for the throw-in. Ronaldinho claimed it was *"luck"*, but it turned out to be a match-winning assist for Atletico Mineiro.[61]

DD23 UNJUST RETURN

DD23 DARK ART DESCRIPTION: When a goalkeeper has possession of the ball and boots it out of the pitch so that a player (either a teammate or opposition player) can receive treatment, the

expected sporting convention is to return the ball directly back to the keeper's possession.

But this dark art disregards *"like for like"*. Teams that were not in possession will subtly exploit this situation. On restart (i.e. from their throw in) they will put the ball out over the goal line (for a goal kick) or, better still, sometimes on the touchline near the corner flag (for a throw-in).

BENEFIT/CONSEQUENCES: This unjust return is not exactly the same as the original situation where the goalkeeper had the ball in his hands. Therefore, the team without possession has sneakily gained a slight edge. The odd thing is that players and supporters usually clap to show their appreciation of the unjust return despite the ball not being returned directly to the goalkeeper's possession.

DD24 UNJUST GOAL BY RETURN

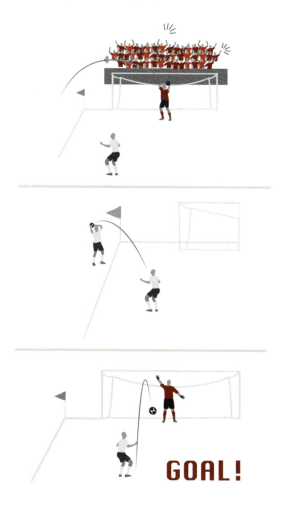

DD24 DARK ART DESCRIPTION: This is when a team is expected to return the ball to the opposition at restart (as in **DD23 Unjust Return**), but instead they retain possession and score a goal. When a goal is scored from this situation, the scorer will always plead

innocent but nevertheless will be pleased he has helped his team score an unjust and unsporting goal.[62, 63]

VARIATION: When an injured goalkeeper has possession of the ball, but he cannot kick or throw the ball out of the pitch and just releases the ball on the ground, an opponent takes control of the ball and scores a goal.

ONLINE SEARCH: *"most unfair goal in football history"*; *"Arsenal 2-1 Sheffield United (1998-99) FA Cup result void"*; *"Luis Adriano no fair play"*.

DD25 BOGUS BACKSPIN TOSS

DD25 DARK ART DESCRIPTION: A team is awarded a free kick, and the player positions the ball far away from the free kick's real location. The player will usually lob the ball with two hands, appearing to exert some backspin, but the ball usually carries on forward for several metres with no backspin to bring the ball back. Players usually steal distance like this when they have a restart in their own half (such as from an offside call or from a careless foul as in **DD11 Clumsy Tactical Foul**).

VARIATION: Players can test the referee's resolve by moving the ball forward at free kicks when they are in the opponent's half of the pitch.

ONLINE SEARCH: *"Referees can exercise discretion on free kick placements".*

This online newspaper article by the author is about *"knowing your percentages on the pitch".* It explains why good referees are not too strict about players stealing distance depending on where the free kick is located on the pitch.[64]

DISRESPECTFUL DARK ARTS

"There has been, over the years, an increase in attempts to manipulate the referee, such as players crowding around the referees, and it can't do the referee's confidence any good – you're undermining his authority. The backing-off process and respect of decisions is a step we hope will improve the quality of referees and the game itself."

—Alex Ferguson[65]

And yet, the greatest British manager of the modern game Sir Alex Ferguson, continued to disrespect, argue with, and undermine referees all the way until his retirement in 2013.

Alex Ferguson

Disrespecting match officials to manipulate or, in some cases, to intimidate them is a dark art that players, managers, fans, and even club owners continue to execute.

ONLINE SEARCH:*"PAOK owner gun".*

Look at the case of a gun-toting PAOK club owner in Greece's Superleague who attempted to approach the referee over an offside call that he found unfavourable.[66] The club owner, Georgian-born Russian Savvidis, is believed to have threatened the referee, saying: *"You're over."*

DD26 RILE THE REFEREE

DD26 DARK ART DESCRIPTION: Whenever a decision goes against a team, players and coaches must question the referee. Always surround and challenge the referee or assistant referee. Players and coaches will forcefully appeal for throw-ins, goal kicks, and corner kicks with the knowledge that they are hoping to trick the match officials into deciding in their favour. Also, it is believed this is a psychological ploy to influence future decisions in their favour, but there is no real evidence for this.

VARIATIONS: Players take turns to whine and whinge at the referee.

BENEFIT/CONSEQUENCES: What players don't understand is that constant whining and complaining actually makes referees disregard their opinions. Referees have the thickest skins. Constant whiners are like little boys who *cry wolf* and have lost all integrity and credibility.

DD27 UP THE ASSISTANT REFEREE

DD27 DARK ART DESCRIPTION: Substitutes are permitted to warm up on the touchlines. Sometimes substitutes can warm up right behind where the assistant referee (AR) runs the line, and even distract him on any offside calls and throw-ins against their own teammates. Substitutes can say things like: *"Hey Lino, our ball"*, *"Foul", Offside"*.

VARIATIONS: Use assistant coaches to *"Have a word"*.

BENEFIT/CONSEQUENCES: There is no benefit to be gained from complaining about a referee's decision, especially when play has moved on. However, the hope here is to psychologically influence or intimidate the assistant referee to think twice about making a decision that goes against their team.

ONLINE SEARCH: *"Warnock"*.

In the documentary about manager Neil Warnock, he gets annoyed with the match officials and gives instructions to his assistant coach to *"have a word with the lino"*. Warnock enjoys criticising match officials.[67]

ONLINE SEARCH: *"Morata assistant referee flag"*.

Chelsea's Alvaro Morata shows petulance by disrespecting the AR's decision.[68]

DD28 FLATTER THE REF

DD28 DARK ART DESCRIPTION: A player or coach will compliment the referee when decisions are given. Even decisions that are against his team are praised, and these are always very clear-cut to dispute. The aim of course is to mislead the referee into thinking the player or coach is a *"nice guy"* and *"very fair-minded"*. That is the intention since the same player or coach will later loudly claim for a penalty or free kick when he or a teammate has fallen from slight physical contact by an opponent.

VARIATIONS: Complimenting, joking around with, and saying pleasant things about the referee at pre-match media conferences and before the match starts. Anything to try to curry favour from the referee! Some clubs or competition organisers even give gifts and souvenirs to match officials *"to sweeten them up"*.[69]

BENEFIT/CONSEQUENCES:

Sneaky players and coaches may think they are playing the referee, but experienced match officials will know that all players and coaches are biased, and therefore will not trust them when making decisions on the pitch. Nevertheless, taken to its logical conclusion, the extreme form of this kind of flattery leads to match fixing, whereby corrupt referees have been known to influence match results in return for bribes.

DD29 DISRESPECT THE MATCH OFFICIALS

DD29 DARK ART DESCRIPTION: It doesn't matter what match officials think; it's what YOU think that matters! Always call *"my ball"* when an opponent has the ball near the touchline or goal line, even if the whole ball has not gone out over the line.

Always shout *"handball"* when a ball strikes an opponent anywhere above the knee area, to con the referee. Always yell *"corner"* when the ball crosses the opposition's goal line.

VARIATIONS: Whenever your team concedes a goal, shout loudly and claim an infringement like *"handball"*, *"foul"* or *"offside"*.

BENEFIT/CONSEQUENCES: By constantly making match officials have *"second thoughts"* about their decisions, players and coaches believe they will distract, weaken, and influence future decisions.

There are many ways to show disdain and disrespect to match officials. Coaches like Mourinho will often stand outside of or leave the technical area. They know the fourth official can only tell them to go back, and this does not have to happen immediately.

However, it is all done to put psychological pressure on the fourth official, so that when an incident occurs that goes against his team, it gives coaches like Mourinho greater power over the match officials. Undermining the authority of match officials is all part of the dark arts.

DD30 PSYCHE OUT THE REF

DD30 DARK ART DESCRIPTION: A star player or manager's pre-match comments about a referee may be enough to psyche out match officials. It is not uncommon for managers to air concerns about the appropriateness of referees, such as the perceived bias of referees and questioning their integrity.

BENEFIT/CONSEQUENCES: Competition organisers can fine players and managers for their pre-match comments about match officials. In 2016, Mourinho at Manchester United attempted to psyche out referee Anthony Taylor and was subsequently fined £50,000 and given a one-match ban.[70, 71]

ONLINE SEARCH: *"Anthony Taylor Mourinho".*

In this example of psyching out the referee, Mourinho suggested the fuss and media attention about the appointment of Anthony Taylor could affect the referee's performance in the upcoming league match between Liverpool and Manchester United.

3 CLEVER CAUTIONS

Oftentimes we see players who deliberately want to get a yellow card. The reason for this calculated action is so the cautioned player will have accumulated the required disciplinary points to miss the next match, which is usually a non-vital game. In doing so, the *"slate"* is wiped clean and the player has eliminated the risk of missing an important future match should there be an unexpected caution.

Problems arise when players do not know the best ways to pick up a yellow card. Because players mainly learn the rules by intuition, all they have to guide them is an understanding based on personal experience and observation. Players will have seen referees award many yellow cards for rough, tough, and late challenges and will assume this is the usual way to get cautioned. From a player's intuition, it seems making a bad tackle and injuring an opponent are necessary requirements for being awarded a yellow card. The trouble is players forget that there are other, safer ways to getting cautioned.

Technically, referees caution players for unfair challenges that are considered *"reckless"*. Therefore, in trying to get cautioned by making a foul on an opponent, the risk is that the player's tackle is rougher than planned and can result in a straight red card. Coaches don't exactly help players when they instruct them to *"go get a yellow card"* without explicitly advising how to go about it.

David Beckham's deliberate yellow is a good example of how not to do it. In an England versus Wales international match in 2004, Beckham needed a yellow card to trigger an automatic suspension. A caution was convenient because it meant the England captain would miss the next international match against lowly Azerbaijan while he recovered from his current rib injury. At that time, the England manager was Sven Goran Eriksson who appeared to leave it up to Beckham to decide how to get a yellow card.

To do so, Beckham deliberately kicked Ben Thatcher to claim his caution for committing a "reckless challenge". It could have easily turned nasty; either Beckham's opponent could have been seriously injured or the opponent could have retaliated violently toward Beckham. Since Beckham was also carrying a rib injury, any physical confrontation with opposition players could have aggravated his injury. Therefore, it would have been smarter to choose a less risky way of picking up a caution.

Moreover, obtaining deliberate *"cheap yellow cards"* is considered *"unsporting"*, and the game's authorities—FIFA and the FA—both publicly criticized Beckham for tarnishing the game's image. Beckham later apologized for his actions. In truth, the dark arts will always be present in the game, and it is up to the lawmakers to mete out punishment that is adequate enough to limit the continued use of unsporting actions.[72, 73]

ONLINE SEARCH: *"deliberate yellow cards"*; *"Arnold told players to get yellow cards"*.

In Australia's A-League, manager Graham Arnold tells his players to get yellow cards.[74]

Realistically, getting a *"cheap caution"* will remain in the game. So, aside from hacking down opponents, this section offers other options for players to deliberately obtain yellow cards without any risk of hurting opponents or themselves. All that is needed is a little knowledge of the rules!

ONLINE SEARCH: *"Mourinho Alonso Ramos yellow card"*.

Players at Spanish club Real Madrid, managed and coached by Mourinho, demonstrated good knowledge of the rules to deliberately get yellow cards and even red cards.[75, 76] Although considered unsporting conduct, these are actually clever examples demonstrating how players can obtain *"easy yellows"* without any risk of injuring themselves or their opponents.

Here are 25 clever and risk-free ways to get cautions.

A. DELIBERATELY DELAYING OWN RESTART

A1. For a throw-in, perform **TW5 Faker Taker Throw-In** (get ready, set, then drop the ball and leave to get cautioned)

A2. For a throw-in, perform **TW7 Throw-In Fingerpointer.** Repeat to get cautioned.

A3. For a goal kick, corner kick, or free kick, perform the **TW9 Stop-and-Think Kick.** Repeat to get cautioned.

A4. At a goal kick, the player who wants a caution should go to take the kick. The player can deliberately do **TW13 Goal Kick Placement Puzzle** with **TW14 Goal Kick Eagle Eyes,** which clearly delays restart and frustrates opponents. Repeat to get yellow card.

B. DELIBERATELY FORCING OWN RETAKE

B1. For a free kick, perform **DD25 Bogus Backspin Toss** to position the ball in the wrong place to force a retake. Repeat to get yellow card.

B2. For a throw-in, perform **TW6 Throw-In Not In** to ensure the ball does not enter the pitch and force a retake. Repeat to get yellow card.

C. HANDBALL HANKY PANKY

C1. Handball. A player must clearly attempt to score a goal against the opposition with his hand (deliberate handball). Even if the goal attempt fails, the referee will have no choice but to give a yellow card.

Note: this is different to using hands to stop a ball from entering a player's own goal (which is a red card offence for DOGSO*).

C2. Handball. A player can use their hand to break up an attacking move (make sure there is another teammate nearby, otherwise it is a red card offence for DOGSO*).

* DOGSO means Denying an Obvious Goal-Scoring Opportunity

D. DELAYING OPPOSITION'S RESTART

D1. Kick the ball away or carry the ball away when a free kick is awarded to the opposing team.

D2. At an opponent's restart, pick up the ball and give it to the referee (who clearly does not want the ball). In return, the referee will caution the player.

D3. When an opponent is about to restart (e.g. from a free kick, corner kick, or throw in), the player should stand next to the ball on the pitch or on the touchline right next to the thrower. When the opponent kicks the ball, the player should quickly move his foot to stop the ball. When the opponent throws the ball, the player should jump up to try to block the ball. The referee will caution the player for not moving away to the required distance.

D4. When an opponent goalkeeper is about to restart with a goal kick, the player should either stand inside the penalty area or quickly enter the area while the ball is simultaneously leaving the area. If the goalkeeper complains to the referee and the referee orders a retake, the player can repeat this action until the referee cautions him (for delaying the restart). If the goalkeeper decides to take a quick goal kick, the player can intercept the ball inside the penalty area and force the referee to issue a yellow card.

E. OFFENCE ENTERING OR LEAVING PITCH

E1. A player can walk off the pitch without telling the referee and will be cautioned when he publicly asks for permission to re-enter the pitch.

E2. A player can ask for the referee's permission to seek medical treatment off the pitch or change his equipment or boots. Next, without publicly telling the referee, the player re-enters the pitch and will collect a caution.

E3. A player, when being substituted, will slowly leave the pitch and deliberately not leave the field at the nearest point on the boundary line (**TW21 Super-Slow Sub**). He can make more of a show by approaching the referee to shake his hand. If the referee deems this to be excessive, he will issue a yellow card.

F. DISSENT AGAINST MATCH OFFICIALS

F1. At a free kick, question the referee about the wall distance. Do not restart until the referee is forced to check the distance.

ONLINE SEARCH: *"David Beckham killing time".*

F2. Show dissent at the referee (**Note:** do NOT swear, spit, or use abusive gestures!). Dissent can take various non-aggressive forms, such as taking his pen or cards, pretending to throw the ball at him, or disagreeing with him by wagging a finger at his decisions.

F3. Show dissent at the assistant referee (AR) by purposely running some distance toward him to vent anger and frustration.

F4. When the referee uses a marker spray, immediately and deliberately wipe away the foam to earn a yellow card.

F5. If the competition uses Video Assistant Referees (VARs), a player can show dissent by regularly urging the referee to video review his decisions just to undermine his authority. The player needs to constantly make the signal of a TV screen for a video review.

G. FOR GOAL-SCORERS ONLY

G1. Score and then take off their shirt.

G2. Score and then jump over the perimeter fence or boundary, or even into the spectators.

G3. Score and then incite the opposition fans; for instance by *"cupping an ear to them"* to suggest they have been silenced and muted by the goal.

Note: do NOT use offensive, insulting or abusive gestures.

H. PITCH ISSUES

H1. Make an unauthorized mark on the pitch (or deliberately destroy the penalty mark). Perform **DD21 Grass Cutter** and make it obvious.

H2. Remove the corner flag from its upright position and throw it on the ground.

CONCLUSION

THE BEAUTIFUL GAME DOES NOT EXIST IN ISOLATION

No one is quite sure where the term *the Beautiful Game* originated, although almost everyone accepts this positive-sounding term describes football at its best.

Officially, Brazilian great Pelé used it in his 1977 autobiography *My Life and the Beautiful Game,* using the Portuguese phrase *O Jogo Bonito.*[77] Also, English TV commentator Stuart Hall used it further back in 1958 to describe the attractive style of Manchester City's Peter Doherty.

However, it is likely that the term was kicking around much earlier and entered the lexicon—probably through different languages and cultures—as the game ballooned in popularity, professionalism, and commercialism. What is clear is the term *the Beautiful Game* succinctly captures the sport's complete aesthetic, idealistic and mesmerizing qualities.

People either believe in or wish the sport to be *"beautiful"* while at the same time ignoring or refusing to acknowledge that the game is also brutal, ugly, and vicious. This overriding belief in *the Beautiful Game* is seen in many advertising commercials.

For instance, sportswear company Nike uses the *"good vs evil"* concept in many guises, notably in 1996, 2000, and 2014. Such ads showcase the good, positive, and light side of football ultimately triumphing over the bad, negative, and dark aspects of the game. They, along with many other companies, clubs, and individuals, all promote *the Beautiful Game* and its romantic, idealistic values.

The main moral message espoused to everyone is *"it doesn't pay to be bad and unsporting"*. We must love *the Beautiful Game* and it will ultimately triumph over the dirty, evil and unpleasant aspects of football.

But this is too simplistic, especially when you look at "beautiful" teams who have missed out on the ultimate prizes. Former Arsenal forward Emmanuel Adebayor saw this in his manager Arsene Wenger's approach. *"We were nice. We had a gentlemen team. We play, we pass around but when it comes to being dirty, we couldn't,"* said Adebayor.[78] Even Jürgen Klopp, whose Liverpool side lost the 2018 UEFA Champions League in unpleasant circumstances to Real Madrid acknowledged that teams will use the dark arts to win: *"Go there and put an elbow to the goalkeeper, put their goalscorer down like a wrestler in midfield and then you win."* Klopp was specifically referring to Sergio Ramos and his dark arts applied to Liverpool goalkeeper Loris Karius (who appeared concussed from Ramos' elbow to his head, which led to an uncharacteristic goalkeeping error) and to star striker Mohamed Salah (who had to be substituted off after Ramos deliberately locked arms and injured Salah's shoulder).[78]

Without the bad, ugly, and nasty side of football, there would be no ideal to aim for in the first place. For every Pelé, Lionel Messi, Cristiano Ronaldo and any aesthetically pleasing team that light up the pitch in glory, there are thousands more journeymen players and hard-grafting teams who ply their trade in an unappealing and unattractive manner.

What is not known or is quickly dismissed about these lower-profile players is that they are winners in their own right. They may not have the best skills, best speed, or best physiques, but what they do have is the know-how and mental toughness in getting the job done. Ashley

Barnes, a successful journeyman player at Burnley admitted to using the dark arts on players, especially on talented opponents: *"I do like to wind up the big teams, and sometimes they fall for it, sometimes not. Of course I enjoy playing the villain. They're 10 times better than you on the pitch so you've got to try and bring them down, or try some tactic to get the upper hand."*[79]

Players like Barnes are survivors, have durability, and ultimately they become winners because they know about the dark arts.

This book aims to bring attention to the unheralded, unpleasant, and unattractive side of football, not to promote the use of the dark arts, but to bring more awareness to this part of *the Beautiful Game*. Looking beyond the ungentlemanly and unsporting conduct of the dark arts, there is in truth some *"beauty"* in identifying them because it opens up the real world of football and gives all stakeholders a wider and deeper appreciation of all types of people in the game.

Zlatan Ibrahimovic, a self-proclaimed *"warrior player"*, understands the importance of being rough and tough to survive. "*Hatred and revenge*" are the motivators that get him going:

> *"What happens on the pitch stays on the pitch. That's my philosophy and, to be honest, you'd be shocked if you knew what goes on out there. There are punches and insults, it's a constant fight, but to us players it's business as usual. [Inter Milan defenders like Marco Materazzi and Siniša Mihajlović] give you an idea [about the dark arts]. They could play nasty and hard, and it's brutal. It's insults and hate."*

—Zlatan Ibrahimovic[80]

So, at the risk of being shocked, why not open up our eyes and ears to discover more about what really goes on out there on the pitch amongst the players? What does it really take to succeed out on the football pitch?

Dutch master Johan Cruyff is credited with the quote: *"Football is a game you play with your brain"*,[81] and this is evident in many experienced players. Smart players are those who have enough understanding of the game to outplay, outfight, and outwit their opponents, and even outfox match officials. They have what Barcelona legend Xavi Hernandez calls: *"game intelligence"*. This includes knowledge of the dark arts to either exploit opponents or to escape from being exploited. Xavi is a pupil and practitioner of the teachings of Cruyff and throughout his career has always used his brain and game intelligence to express himself positively and to avoid being a victim of the dark arts.

In the 1990s, Cruyff even *"advised"* Alex Ferguson (who had yet to win the European Cup, now called the UEFA Champions League, with Manchester United) on how the dark arts can help his team win Europe's top club competition. The Dutch master observed how English clubs playing in Europe *"don't cheat and don't buy referees"*.[82] Nothing has changed in the intervening 25 years. For instance, this is exactly what transpired in the 2018 UEFA Champions League final, with Real Madrid using the dark arts with aplomb and English club Liverpool, being victims of the dark arts, losing.[78] Nevermind that Liverpool became champions the following year because in that final it was two English clubs (Liverpool and Tottenham Hotspur) competing, and the dark arts did not play any significant role in major incidents.

In football, as in *Life*, the harsh reality is that not everyone obeys the rules. Some people who bend or break the law are caught and disciplined, but many more escape being punished, having found ways to beat the system.

Trying to beat the system is what makes us human. Those who dare to push the boundaries, those who dare to risk without getting caught, and those who discover newer creative loopholes actually help in improving and developing *the Beautiful Game*. Without knowledge of the dark arts, the game's lawmakers would have little to do.

Diving and phantom fouls are dark art examples that have existed long in people's collective memories. These negative acts remain in the game because the punishment for getting caught and disciplined (a yellow card) is small compared with the greater reward of fooling the referee into sending off an opponent and potentially gaining a match-winning penalty.

Referee Mark Clattenburg skilfully dealt with the dark arts and was the world's best referee with his match preparation and player management skills at both the 2016 UEFA Champions League and European Championships finals.[54]

Match officials like Clattenburg who embrace the challenge in learning about and managing the dark arts are the ones who help reduce negative actions on the pitch and promote the beauty of the game.

However, there is only so much match officials can do to combat the dark arts.

Players, assistant coaches, and managers will continue to test the boundaries as long as lawmakers struggle to amend the rules and to effectively punish the practitioners of the dark arts.

For instance, no disciplinary action was taken against the dark arts practitioners in the 2016 Champions League final (two Spanish teams), even though their behaviour clearly failed to uphold the *"spirit, beauty and image"* of the game. If these master practitioners easily escape punishment for their negative actions, while remaining winners and champions, then there will always be those who will bend the rules and beat the system.[54] Real Madrid's Ramos, among others, obviously continues with his dark arts because he knows they have helped him become successful and a serial winner.

Football has come a long way since 1863 when the original set of 14 laws were officially established by a group of ex-public schoolboys in the Freemasons' Tavern, Great Queen Street in London.[83] In that bygone era, where the modern game of football originated at exclusive English public schools, there was an assumption that a gentleman would never ever deliberately commit a foul. This was the ideal, and some would say naïve, version of the game when *"being a good sport"* mattered more than winning. That was over 155 years ago. How times have changed!

With increasingly competitive games, professionalism, and an unhealthy desire to win at all costs, players developed underhanded ways or dark arts to cheat and give themselves better chances to win. Ever since, the rules have always been two or three steps behind the times. The history of the Laws of the Game offers a fascinating view at how the game has developed since 1863. Many of the amendments to the rules came as a consequence of players and coaches using the dark arts to negatively affect the game.

Football develops and improves constantly. With newer trickery, tactics, and technology appearing in the modern game, players will inevitably find new ways to fool opponents and match officials. And lawmakers are kept busy identifying ways to amend the rules to help minimize the use of darks arts.

There is no doubt that *the Beautiful Game* and the *Dark Arts* are forever entwined and will evolve together as long as football exists as a competitive sport and a major commercial industry.

We ignore the dark arts at our peril. Instead we must appreciate the game for what it is: a fascinating mix of positive (light) and negative (dark) forces battling for the ultimate prize of winning.

To truly appreciate the game of football we must learn and understand these two very different aspects of the game, which ultimately bring out the best and the worst in us.

REFERENCES

THE DARK ARTS

1. Gallagher, Danny. *"Manchester United boss Jose Mourinho mixes praise and criticism for Luke Shaw after Everton clash: 'He had a good performance which was his body with my brain'."* MailOnline, 5 Apr. 2017, www.dailymail.co.uk/sport/football/article-4381016/Man-Utd-new-Mourinho-mixes-praise-criticism-Shaw.html

2. Wheeler, Chris. *"Jose Mourinho continues Manchester United blame game as disgruntled boss prepares for mass summer cull."* MailOnline, 18 Mar. 2018, www.dailymail.co.uk/sport/football/article-5516053/Jose-Mourinho-continues-Manchester-United-blame-game.html

3. Kinnersley, Jack. *"'He will learn over the season he needs to do that a lot': Jose Mourinho aims dig at Luke Shaw as he warns Harry Maguire he will need to cover for Manchester United left-back."* MailOnline, 11 Aug 2019, www.dailymail.co.uk/sport/football/article-7346601/Jose-Mourinho-aims-dig-Luke-Shaw-warns-Harry-Maguire.html

4. Gaughan, Jack. *"Jose Mourinho storms out of interview as Manchester United boss takes aim at Jurgen Klopp and Arsene Wenger: 'The rules for me are different'."* MailOnline, 1 Feb. 2017, www.dailymail.co.uk/sport/football/article-4182434/Man-United-manager-Jose-Mourinho-storms-interview.html

5. Law, Matt. *"Jose Mourinho criticises Chelsea doctor Eva Carneiro after Swansea draw."* The Telegraph, 9 Aug. 2015, www.telegraph.co.uk/sport/football/teams/chelsea/11792452/

Jose-Mourinho-criticises-Chelsea-physio-Eva-Carneiro-after-Swansea-draw.html

6. Barclay, Patrick. *"Mourinho. Further Anatomy of a Winner."* Orion 2012, pp 129

7. Kinnersley, Jack. *"Jose Mourinho wanted to kick 'mentally weak' Anthony Martial out of Manchester United."* MailOnline, 27 Aug 2019, www.dailymail.co.uk/sport/football/article-7399493/Manchester-United-news-Jose-Mourinho-wanted-kick-mentally-weak-Anthony-Martial-out.html

8. Todd, Oliver. *"Jose Mourinho lists players he has most enjoyed working with, including Alvaro Arbeloa as a surprise name alongside John Terry, Frank Lampard and Xabi Alonso."* MailOnline, 7 Jun. 2015, www.dailymail.co.uk/sport/football/article-3114221/Jose-Mourinho-lists-players-enjoyed-working-including-Alvaro-Arbeloa-surprise-name.html

9. Bezants, Jack. *"REVEALED: Jose Mourinho's incredible scouting report for Chelsea taking on Barcelona in 2006, focusing on 'constant cheater' Ronaldinho and the 'amazing' 18-year-old Lionel Messi, where the only way to stop him is to kick him!"* MailOnline, 19 Mar. 2019, www.dailymail.co.uk/sport/football/article-6825985/Jose-Mourinhos-incredible-scouting-report-Chelsea-taking-Barcelona-2006.html

TIME-WASTING TACTICS

10. Keown, Martin. *"Chelsea time-wasted against Liverpool at Anfield... but we did the same at Arsenal under George*

Graham!" MailOnline, 28 Apr. 2014, www.dailymail.co.uk/
sport/football/article-2615084/MARTIN-KEOWN-Chelsea-
did-time-waste-against-Liverpool-Anfield-did-Arsenal-George-
Graham.html

11. Bhardwaj, Vaishali. *"West Ham's Mark Noble carries injured Ander Herrera off the pitch during FA Cup loss to Manchester United."* Evening Standard, 14 Apr. 2016, www.standard.co.uk/sport/football/west-hams-mark-noble-carries-injured-ander-herrera-off-the-pitch-during-fa-cup-loss-to-manchester-a3225076.html

12. Innes, Richard. *"Egyptian player carries 'injured' opponent off the pitch - becomes hero to all haters of gamesmanship."* The Mirror, 21 Jun. 2015, www.mirror.co.uk/sport/row-zed/egyptian-player-carries-injured-opponent-5924288

13. Issacs, Marc. *"Former Serbia international Danko Lazovic makes Victor Moses look good with incredible piece of simulation."* The Mirror, 29 May. 2017, www.mirror.co.uk/sport/football/news/victor-moses-danko-lazovic-simulation-10522597

14. Innes, Richard. *"South African player produces the most outrageous showboat in football history."* The Mirror, 9 Mar. 2016, www.mirror.co.uk/sport/row-zed/south-african-player-produces-most-7516904

15. Wilson, Jeremy. *"Chelsea's David Luiz: I was smiling at jeering Manchester United fans, not Rafael's red card."* The Telegraph, 6 May 2013, www.telegraph.co.uk/sport/football/teams/chelsea/10040313/Chelseas-David-Luiz-I-was-smiling-at-jeering-Manchester-United-fans-not-Rafaels-red-card.html

16. *"Goalkeepers are not above the Law."* FIFA News, 31 Oct. 1997, www.fifa.com/news/y=1997/m=10/news=goalkeepers-are-not-above-the-law-72050.html

17. de Menezes, Jack. *"Liverpool 2 Bordeaux 1: Jurgen Klopp trolls Simon Mignolet after goalkeeper's error."* The Independent, 27 Nov. 2015, www.independent.co.uk/sport/football/european/liverpool-2-bordeaux-1-jurgen-klopp-trolls-simon-mignolet-press-conference-goalkeepers-error-a6750976.html

18. Di Salvo, V. *"Activity profile of elite goalkeepers during football match-play."* J Sports Med Phys Fitness. 2008 Dec;48(4):443-6. www.ncbi.nlm.nih.gov/pubmed/18997646

19. Coles, Rebecca. *"WHAT A SIP UP Mark Flekken chooses wrong moment to take a drink from water bottle... as opposition striker nips in to score."* The Sun, 24 Feb. 2018, www.thesun.co.uk/sport/5663101/mark-flekken-fifa-glitch-moment-duisburg-ingolstadt/

20. McCartney, Aidan. *"Teenager charged with assault after football fan jumped onto keeper's back as he put ball down for goal kick."* MailOnline, 5 Feb. 2013, www.dailymail.co.uk/news/article-2273688/Jordan-Archer-attack-Football-fan-arrested-jumping-keepers-ball-goal-kick.html

21. *"South African goalkeeper proves that time wasting can be a waste of time: Video."* The Metro, 19 Sep. 2013, www.metro.co.uk/2013/09/19/south-african-goalkeeper-proves-that-time-wasting-can-be-a-waste-of-time-video-4054797/

22. Anderson, David. *"You are spineless."* The Mirror, 3 Nov. 2008, www.mirror.co.uk/sport/other-sports/you-are-spineless-354662

23. *"Henry: I was riled by timewasting."* MailOnline, 12 Feb. 2007, www.dailymail.co.uk/sport/football/article-435683/Henry-I-riled-timewasting.html

24. Grounds, Ben. *"Senegal goalkeeper Khadim N'Diaye takes time-wasting to a new level as he comically trips over his own feet."* MailOnline, 24 Jan. 2017, www.dailymail.co.uk/sport/football/article-4150788/Senegal-s-Khadim-N-Diaye-takes-time-wasting-new-level.html

25. *"Wayne Rooney shoves Pep Guardiola during Manchester derby as tensions boil over."* Metro, 10 Sep. 2016, www.metro.co.uk/2016/09/10/wayne-rooney-shoves-pep-guardiola-during-manchester-derby-as-tensions-boil-over-6120381/

26. Lai, William. *"Rational Ref: Let's call time on those who run down the clock."* SCMP, 18 Dec. 2014, www.scmp.com/sport/soccer/article/664725/rational-ref-lets-call-time-those-who-run-down-clock

27. Lai, William. *"Alan Pardew is what he is, unfortunately."* SCMP, 13 Mar. 2014, www.scmp.com/sport/soccer/article/1447914/alan-pardew-what-he-unfortunately

28. White, Jim. *"Ballboys in sporting fixtures have much more to do than just waste time."* The Telegraph, 25 Jan. 2013, www.telegraph.co.uk/sport/football/teams/swansea-city/9826874/Ballboys-in-sporting-fixtures-have-much-more-to-do-than-just-waste-time.html

29. Palmer, Bryn. *"Eric Cantona's kung-fu kick: The moment that shocked football."* BBC News, 3 Nov. 2017, www.bbc.com/sport/football/30916435

DEVILISH DECEPTIONS

30. *"Zinedine Zidane will never say sorry to Marco Materazzi for World Cup headbutt as France legend admits: I would rather die."* MailOnline, 1 Mar. 2010, www.dailymail.co.uk/sport/football/article-1254630/Zinedine-Zidane-say-sorry-Marco-Materazzi-World-Cup-headbutt-France-legend-admits-I-die.html

31. Hay, Anthony. *"Liverpool midfielder Emre Can reveals he was given a 'wet willy' during his side's FA Cup draw with Plymouth."* MailOnline, 10 Jan 2017, www.dailymail.co.uk/sport/football/article-4106388/Liverpool-midfielder-Emre-reveals-given-wet-willy-s-FA-Cup-draw-Plymouth.html

32. Prenderville, Liam. *"Watch Gonzalo Jara stick his finger up Edinson Cavani's BACKSIDE during unsavoury Copa America clash."* The Mirror, 25 Jun. 2015, www.mirror.co.uk/sport/football/news/watch-gonzalo-jara-stick-finger-5945101

33. Reddy, Luke. *"Biting, butting, spitting... what is football's deadliest sin?"* BBC, 5 Mar. 2015, www.bbc.com/sport/football/31746786

34. Crafton, Adam. *"How racist abuse sparked his infamous City celebration, the night he almost took his own life and what it's like working with 'beautiful manager' Wenger and 'killer' Mourinho."* MailOnline, 25 Apr. 2019, www.dailymail.co.uk/sport/football/article-6959717/EMMANUEL-ADEBAYOR-EXCLUSIVE-racist-abuse-sparked-celebration-against-Arsenal.html

35. Grounds, Ben. *"Juventus defender Giorgio Chiellini was lucky not to be sent off for elbow on Radamel Falcao, says Glenn Hoddle."*

MailOnline, 3 May 2017, www.dailymail.co.uk/sport/football/article-4471388/Hoddle-Giorgio-Chiellini-lucky-stay-pitch.html

36. Todd, Oliver. *"Bournemouth defender Tyrone Mings hits out at 'upsetting' five-match ban and says stamping on an opponent's head 'would never cross my mind'."* MailOnline, 10 Mar. 2017, www.dailymail.co.uk/sport/football/article-4301842/Tyrone-Mings-hits-upsetting-five-match-ban.html

37. *"Pepe apologises for 'unintentional' stamp on Messi's hand after backlash."* MailOnline, 20 Jan. 2012, www.dailymail.co.uk/sport/football/article-2089132/Pepe-apologises-stamp-Messi.html

38. Griffee, Will. *"'Alexis Sanchez and I didn't used to get on... when he signed I said "Oh, f****** hell no"' admits Marcos Rojo as he reveals Jose Mourinho told him not to kick Chilean in Manchester United training."* MailOnline, 20 Mar. 2018, www.dailymail.co.uk/sport/football/article-5521571/Rojo-reaction-Sanchez-joining-Man-United-F-hell-no.html

39. *"Ronaldinho wins reprieve."* BBC News, 23 Jun. 2002, news.bbc.co.uk/sport3/worldcup2002/hi/team_pages/brazil/newsid_2058000/2058110.stm

40. Polden, Jake. *"Danny Mills reveals how England got Ronaldinho sent off in 2002 World Cup - with the help of Paul Scholes."* The Mirror, 16 Dec. 2016, www.mirror.co.uk/sport/football/news/danny-mills-reveals-how-england-9467824

41. Keown, Martin. *"Martin Keown: This is how Liverpool should handle Chelsea's Diego Costa."* Daily Express, 15 Sep. 2016,

www.express.co.uk/sport/football/711184/Martin-Keown-Diego-Costa-Chelsea-Liverpool-Premier-League-preview

42. Bassam, Tom. *"'Dele Alli could have finished the fella's career': Ex-Tottenham boss Harry Redknapp slams horror tackle."* MailOnline, 23 Feb. 2017, www.dailymail.co.uk/sport/football/article-4254398/Dele-Alli-ended-career-says-Harry-Redknapp.html

43. Winters, Max. *"Wayne Rooney opens up on why Alexis Sanchez is 'perfect' for Manchester United, arguing with Roy Keane over The X Factor and getting Cristiano Ronaldo sent off at the 2006 World Cup during Monday Night Football."* MailOnline, 5 Feb. 2018, www.dailymail.co.uk/sport/football/article-5354949/Wayne-Rooney-appears-Monday-Night-Football.html

44. Bascombe, Chris. *"Leicester manager Claudio Ranieri dragged away from referee after Jamie Vardy red sparks Foxes' fury."* The Telegraph, 17 Dec. 2016, www.telegraph.co.uk/football/2016/12/17/leicester-manager-claudio-ranieri-dragged-away-referee-jamie/

45. Wilson, Jeremy and Winter, Henry. *"Patrick Battiston still haunted by Harald Schumacher's brutal foul in France's 1982 Tragedy of Seville."* The Telegraph, 3 Jul. 2014, www.telegraph.co.uk/sport/football/teams/france/10942263/Patrick-Battiston-still-haunted-by-Harald-Schumachers-brutal-foul-in-Frances-1982-Tragedy-of-Seville.html

46. Bernstein, Joe. *"Jose Mourinho accuses Manchester City of strategic fouling as United boss draws attention to tactical ploy ahead of derby: 'The referee has to do his job'."* MailOnline, 9 Dec.

2017, www.dailymail.co.uk/sport/football/article-5163315/ Jose-Mourinho-accuses-Manchester-City-strategic-fouling.html

47. Smyth, Rob. *"Why the Makelele foul is the real threat to football."* The Guardian, 27 Mar. 2008, www.theguardian.com/ football/2008/mar/27/sport.comment3

48. Smith, Adam. *"Atletico Madrid boss Diego Simeone faces three-match ban after being sent to stands for appearing to encourage boy to throw extra ball on pitch during win over Malaga."* MailOnline, 25 Apr. 2016, http://www.dailymail. co.uk/sport/football/article-3556142/Atletico-Madrid-boss-Diego-Simeone-faces-three-match-ban-sent-stands-appearing-encourage-boy-throw-extra-ball-pitch-win-Malaga.html

49. *"Highbury tunnel players in clear."* BBC News, 2 Feb. 2005, http://news.bbc.co.uk/sport2/hi/football/eng_ prem/4228397.*stm*

50. Lowe, Sid. *"Lionel Messi capitalises for Barcelona as Real Madrid see red again."* The Guardian, 27 Apr. 2011, www.theguardian. com/football/2011/apr/27/real-madrid-barcelona-champions-league

51. Rosenblatt, Ryan. *"This is one of the most exaggerated, hilarious fake injuries you will see."* Fox Sports, 28 May 2017, https:// www.foxsports.com/soccer/story/this-is-one-of-the-most-exaggerated-hilarious-fake-injuries-you-will-see-052817

52. Hayward, Paul. *"Thomas Müller not to blame for Pepe's headbutt during Germany's 4-0 win over Portugal."* The Telegraph, 16 Jun. 2014, www.telegraph.co.uk/sport/football/world-

cup/10904106/Thomas-Muller-not-to-blame-for-Pepes-
headbutt-during-Germanys-4-0-win-over-Portugal.html

53. Bernstein, Joe. *"Burnley 0-1 Lincoln City: Sean Raggett heads
    home dramatic late winner as Danny Cowley's giant-killers make
    FA Cup history at Turf Moor."* MailOnline, 19 Feb. 2017, www.
    dailymail.co.uk/sport/football/article-4237372/Burnley-0-1-
    Lincoln-City-Sean-Raggett-heads-home-winner.

54. Ingle, Sean. *"Time to introduce the Pepe Rule after his
    Champions League final antics."* The Guardian, 29 May 2016,
    www.theguardian.com/football/blog/2016/may/29/why-it-
    is-time-football-introduced-the-pepe-rule

55. Critchley, Mark. *"Roy Keane slams diving Ashley Young as 'an
    absolute disgrace' after Manchester United's Champions League
    win."* The Independent, 5 Nov. 2015, www.independent.co.uk/
    sport/football/european/roy-keane-slams-diving-ashley-
    young-as-an-absolute-disgrace-after-manchester-uniteds-
    champions-a6722041.html

56. Taylor, Daniel. *"José Mourinho criticises Old Trafford fans
    for giving Scott McTominay stick."* The Guardian, 10 Mar.
    2018,   www.theguardian.com/football/2018/mar/10/jose-
    mourinho-blasts-old-trafford-crowd-for-giving-scott-mctominay-
    stick

57. Vecsey, George. *"Maradona Has Arm (Maybe) In Victory."* The New
    York Times, 14 Jun. 1990, www.nytimes.com/1990/06/14/
    sports/maradona-has-arm-maybe-in-victory.html

58. *"Maradona: VAR would have disallowed my goal against
    England."* FIFA, 25 Jul. 2017, www.fifa.com/about-fifa/news/

y=2017/m=7/news=maradona-var-would-have-disallowed-my-goal-against-england-2901486.html

59. Davis, Callum. *"Ajax defender Joel Veltman produces the most unsportsmanlike move of all time."* The Telegraph, 13 Feb. 2017, www.telegraph.co.uk/football/2017/02/12/ajax-defender-joel-veltman-produces-unsportsmanlike-move-time/

60. Christenson, Marcus. *"Hitz and miss: Augsburg keeper apologises for sabotaging penalty spot."* The Guardian, 6 Dec. 2015, www.theguardian.com/football/2015/dec/06/augsburg-goalkeeper-tampers-penalty-spot-miss-cologne

61. Drayton, John. *"Ronaldinho shows how to create a goal despite appearing 20 YARDS OFFSIDE using only a bottle of water."* MailOnline, 18 Feb. 2013, www.dailymail.co.uk/sport/football/article-2280404/Ronaldinho-sets-Atletico-Mineiro-goal-despite-appearing-20-yards-offside-position.html

62. Kent, David. *"Charged! Shakhtar striker Adriano hit by UEFA rap over unsporting goal in Denmark."* MailOnline, 21 Nov. 2012, www.dailymail.co.uk/sport/football/article-2236407/Luiz-Adriano-charged-UEFA-unsporting-goal-Shakhtar-Donetsk-v-Nordsjaelland.html

63. Moore, Glenn. *"Football: FA right to follow Wenger's lead."* The Independent, 15 Feb. 1999, www.independent.co.uk/sport/football-fa-right-to-follow-wengers-lead-1070957.html

64. Lai, William. *"Referees can exercise discretion on free kick ball placement."* SCMP, 23 Jan. 2015 www.scmp.com/sport/soccer/article/1689299/referees-can-exercise-discretion-free-kick-ball-placement

65. Winter, Henry. *"Manchester United boss Sir Alex Ferguson is a great manager, but sets bad example with ugly tirades."* The Telegraph, 28 Dec. 2012, www.telegraph.co.uk/sport/football/teams/manchester-united/9768356/Manchester-United-boss-Sir-Alex-Ferguson-is-a-great-manager-but-sets-bad-example-with-ugly-tirades.html

66. Smith, Helena. *"Greek Superleague suspended after team owner invades pitch with a gun."* The Guardian, 12 Mar. 2018, www.theguardian.com/football/2018/mar/12/greek-football-match-stopped-after-team-owner-invades-pitch-with-a-gun

67. Warnock, Neil. *"The Gaffer: The Trials and Tribulations of a Football Manager."* Headline, 2014

68. Lewis, Darren. *"Antonio Conte to warn Chelsea striker Alvaro Morata to clean up his act: This is a situation we can improve'."* The Mirror, 11 Mar. 2018, www.mirror.co.uk/sport/football/news/antonio-conte-warn-chelsea-striker-12170632

69. Lai, William. *"Receiving goodies an ugly scourge of the FIFA executives' game."* SCMP, 25 Sep. 2014, www.scmp.com/sport/soccer/article/1600408/receiving-goodies-ugly-scourge-fifa-executives-game

70. Bernstein, Joe. *"Mourinho: It will be difficult for ref Anthony Taylor to perform well in Liverpool vs Manchester United clash."* MailOnline, 16 Oct. 2016, www.dailymail.co.uk/sport/football/article-3840068/Jose-Mourinho-difficult-ref-Anthony-Taylor-perform-Liverpool-vs-Manchester-United-clash.html

71. Lovett, Samuel. *"Manchester United: Jose Mourinho fined £50,000 and hit with one-match ban following FA double*

charge." The Independent, 2 Nov. 2016, www.independent. co.uk/sport/football/premier-league/manchester-united- jose-mourinho-fined-50000-anthony-taylor-remarks- misconduct-a7394266.html

CLEVER CAUTIONS

72. *"Beckham escapes FA booking charge."* BBC News, 21 Oct. 2004, news.bbc.co.uk/sport1/hi/football/internationals/3754942.stm

73. *"Beckham sorry for deliberate yellow card."* The Telegraph, 13 Oct. 2004, www.telegraph.co.uk/sport/2388338/Beckham- sorry-for-deliberate-yellow-card.html

74. Larkin, Steve. *"Graham Arnold tells players to get yellow cards."* Sydney Morning Herald, 3 Apr. 2017, www.smh.com.au/ sport/soccer/graham-arnold-tells-players-to-get-yellow-cards- 20170403-gvcn5w.html

75. *"José Mourinho and Real Madrid four charged with unsporting conduct."* The Guardian, 25 Nov. 2010, www.theguardian. com/football/2010/nov/25/jose-mourinho-real-madrid- unsporting-conduct

76. Whitwell, Laurie. *"Is Mourinho up to his old tricks? Just like 2010, Alonso and Ramos booked for dissent... but did they do it on purpose to miss the second leg?"* MailOnline, 4 Apr. 2013, www.dailymail.co.uk/sport/football/article-2303836/Real- Madrids-Sergio-Ramos-Xabi-Alonso-accused-getting-deliberate- yellow-cards.html

CONCLUSION

77. Pele with Fish, Robert L. *"Pele, My Life and the Beautiful Game"*. Doubleday, 1977

78. King, Dominic. *"'Sergio Ramos is ruthless and brutal… I hold him responsible': Liverpool boss Jurgen Klopp slams Real Madrid defender for 'wrestling' move on Mo Salah in Champions League final."* MailOnline, 28 Jul. 2018, www.dailymail.co.uk/sport/football/article-6000649/Jurgen-Klopp-slams-Sergio-Ramos-wrestling-Mo-Salah.html

79. Bernstein, Joe. *"Is this man Liverpool's last hope? Anfield fans are banking on Ashley Barnes… but the striker's son is praying for Manchester City!"* MailOnline, 28 Apr. 2019, www.dailymail.co.uk/sport/football/article-6967417/Anfield-fans-banking-Ashley-Barnes-son-praying-Manchester-City.html

80. Ibrahimovic, Zlatan with Lagercrantz, David. *"I Am Zlatan Ibrahimovic"*. Penguin Books, 2013. Translated from the Swedish by Ruth Urbom

81. Winner, David. *"Brilliant Orange: The Neurotic Genius of Dutch Soccer."* Overlook Press, 2008

82. Ferguson, Alex. *"My Autobiography."* Hodder, 2014, pp258-259

83. *"From 1863 to the Present Day."* FIFA, accessed 19 Mar. 2018, www.fifa.com/about-fifa/who-we-are/the-laws/index.html

ABOUT THE AUTHOR

William Lai is a university lecturer, media columnist, and referee in Hong Kong, China. He has also refereed in England and Australia, and is a qualified referee instructor and assessor. He teaches a popular undergraduate course *"Managing Soccer Clubs in a Globalised World"* to management students, comments as *"The Rational Ref"* about football incidents on and off the pitch in Hong Kong's top English-language newspaper, and officiates in Hong Kong's Premier League. He loves to observe, play, officiate, and comment on the good, the bad, and the ugly sides of football.

Cover and interior design: Anja Elsen
Illustrations: JoJo Chin
Layout: Amnet Services

Managing editor: Elizabeth Evans
Copyeditor: Joshua Brazee